Sheridan College

P9-API-875

Now What?

readings on surviving (and even enjoying) your first experience at college teaching

Second Edition

The Teaching Assistant Program
of the Graduate School
Syracuse University

Joseph Janes &
Diane Hauer

Developed in
The Center for Instructional Development
Syracuse University

Copley Publishing Group
Littleton, Massachusetts 01460

© 1988 by Syracuse University. All rights reserved.

Printed in the United States of America.

ISBN 0-87411-214-1

Table of Contents

Preface

This is a book of readings. Books of readings tend to be dry, lifeless, and let's face it, a little dull. To put this together, we've spent a lot of time reading through manuals on teaching, newsletters, reports, and books, culling what we felt were the best, most useful pieces on many aspects of the teaching process. Now our challenge is to assemble these bits and pieces into a meaningful whole.

We've tried to do this in three ways: first, by the organization of the subjects within the book. We have placed up front information on the general aspects of teaching that many people face: lecturing, leading a discussion, questioning, grading, self-evaluation, etc. In the second part, we have readings on "special topics:" selections to refer to when a problem arises, or suggestions on how to improve your basic skills. Here you will find material on humor in the classroom, office hours, writing letters of recommendation, syllabus preparation, and so forth. To help you, we've also included an extensive index at the back to assist in tracking down information which cuts across our divisions.

The second way we've tried to unify the thrust and tone of the book is through our three teaching assistants, Steve, Maureen, and Mercedes. They represent various levels of experience, background, subject matter, and responsibilities of TAs. We hope that the problems and challenges they face, and their discussions and suggestions will tie in with the reading selections to make the topics more real for you.

Finally, at the end of each topic section, we've included a brief summary of the points discussed in the readings. These can serve as a ready reference as questions arise during your teaching.

Of course, since we've collected these items from many sources, from time to time their advice and counsel about some aspects of teaching will differ. We've made no attempt to resolve these questions; rather, we believe their conflicting perspectives serve to point out interesting dilemmas every college teacher faces. Since there is no single "best" solution, take what advice sounds reasonable to you and try it.

We suggest you read this book twice: once before you begin to teach to get a feel for the way things work and give yourself some confidence before you begin. Then, after a few weeks of teaching, go back through it again. There will be things you see in a different light after some teaching experience. In addition, when problems or questions arise, use the index to find out what pearls of wisdom we have to offer.

This effort is part of a larger one; these readings have been assembled to be a part of the Syracuse University Teaching Assistant Program, inaugurated in August 1987. We hope, however, that it will go farther, and that other teaching assistants, and indeed anyone teaching at the college level will find this book helpful and enlightening. We certainly have learned much from this project.

We should note at this point that nothing in this publication is to be construed in any way as the official policy of Syracuse University. Our intent is to provide a variety of perspectives on teaching from people at many institutions.

Our best wishes to all who read this—we hope your teaching improves, and that you enjoy the experience of teaching more, as a result of our efforts. Good luck!

Joseph Janes
Diane Hauer

Syracuse, NY
January, 1988

Acknowledgements

We'd like to thank several people for their assistance and patience during the work on this book.

First, and most importantly, thanks to the original authors of the pieces collected here. Their work is the best we could find, and we thank them for their hard work and their kind permission to use it. They include: Cathy Cohn and Jane Buckley (Syracuse); Andrew Cotton (University of Waterloo); Frederick Crews; Barbara Gross Davis (University of California at Berkeley); Nancy Diamond, Grey Sharp, and John Ory (University of Illinois at Urbana-Champaign); Melvin A. Eggers (Syracuse); Donald Ely (Syracuse); Frank Funk (Syracuse); Vernon Gerlach; Holliday Heine, Peggy Richardson, Arthur Mattuck, Edwin Taylor, Stewart Brown, Allen Olsen and Craig Russell (Massachusetts Institute of Technology); Lee Humphreys and Barbara Wickersham (University of Tennessee at Knoxville); Carl Hurley (Eastern Kentucky University); Sally Jorgensen (Old Dominion University); Katherine Loheyde (Cornell University); Richard Morrow (UCLA); Sandra Napell; John C. Ory (University of Illinois at Urbana-Champaign); Stacy Palmer; Joyce Povlacs (University of Nebraska-Lincoln); Sidney P. Rollins (Bryant College); Sharon Rubin; Robert A. Wolke (University of Pittsburgh) and Jane Woodhead (University of Waterloo).

Next, we thank the Steering Committee of the Teaching Assistant Program at Syracuse University for their guidance and help in the forming of the book. Special thanks to Rosemary Mink and Robert Diamond, whose proofreading and suggestions were most valuable. Robert Diamond also has our appreciation for the several cartoons he graciously contributed.

Thanks also to Martha Strain, who developed the cover design and some of the original drawings.

Double thanks to June Mermigos, who typed vital pieces of this book under extreme pressures placed on her by two unnamed hysterical graduate students, and who we forgot to thank in the first edition (Oops!).

Finally, thanks to our friends: the real people whose names (but not characters) we used in the dialogues. They are all good sports, and we appreciate their cooperation.

J. W. J.
D. M. H.

Introduction

Meet Mercedes, Steve, and Maureen. Mercedes is a second-year graduate student in computer science from Venezuela. Last year she held a teaching assistantship, which involved grading programs and supervising computer lab work. This semester she is teaching a class in the Pascal programming language. Maureen is beginning her third year as a teaching assistant in English, and will be teaching Freshman Composition again this year. Steve is a brand-new TA in History. This year he will be leading a recitation section of about 20 students, grading some exams and papers, and delivering one lecture on the Missouri Compromise.

They meet at a local watering hole, Rosemary's Place, at the beginning of the fall semester, and discover that they're all teaching assistants. They strike up a conversation about the joys and perils of teaching, and become friends. Throughout the semester, they get together from time to time and discuss their classes: how they're going, problems they're having, and what they might like to do better.

They find this informal discussion very helpful. We've printed some of their more fruitful sessions here (don't ask how we got them; hiding under tables is uncomfortable) as introductions to some good readings on the questions and issues they raise.

GETTING UNDER WAY

Part I

1
Preparation

About a week before the semester begins, Mercedes and Maureen are discussing what teaching is like at the college level.

"Do you ever get scared?" asks Mercedes.

"Sure; usually only at the beginning of the semester, though. Once the term has started, and I'm into the groove of teaching, it gets a lot easier. The only times I'm *really* scared after that is when I'm not prepared."

"Does that happen?"

"Not too often after the first time I did it. I've never felt so awful in my life. I had a 20-page paper due at noon, and a lecture to prepare for 9:30. Well, I decided that the paper was more important, so I put off working on the lecture. It took me almost all night to finish the paper, and by 6:00 I couldn't even *think* about sentence structure, let alone write about it. So, I got three hours sleep, scribbled some notes at 9:15, and walked in cold. That was the longest hour of my life. I stammered, I stuttered—I really didn't even know what I was doing. I swore to myself never to do that again."

"Wow. So what do you do now? Write out the complete lecture?"

"No, I can't really work like that. It's not fresh, it's flat, and usually boring. I just think about what I want to do in class, organize my thoughts, and make some notes. Nothing really elaborate, unless it's material I'm not very familiar with. Then I make more detailed notes. But I couldn't read a script. Dull dull dull."

"Hmmm. Thanks a lot. I feel much better now. But I'm still a bit nervous."

"No reason to be," says Maureen with a smile, "you don't start for a week yet."

PREPARATION

When given an opportunity to tell prospective TAs what everybody forgot to tell them, many TAs talk about preparation. Be careful about what you assume to be obvious. An idea may seem trivial to you, when to the student the same concept may be evasive and obscure. Spend time before entering the classroom trying to explain these "obvious" concepts. If you don't, you can bet that when confronted by the students, the result will be embarrassment on your part and a possible insult to the students.

I learned that it is far, far better to be overprepared than underprepared. It was a case of one-trial learning. A most difficult and recurring problem I face, especially teaching a given course or section for the first time, is gauging the amount of material to be covered in any particular class meeting. Clearly, teaching involves a lot of preparation. But how much? I have spent days preparing for a one-hour class in which only 1/5 of what I had prepared was covered. I have also (I guiltily admit) been underprepared because of lack of time—rather, I didn't *make* time for preparation. I have listed what I feel are the consequences of each of these.

BEING OVERPREPARED

1. Anger at myself for not sleeping, skipping lunch before class for further preparation—in short, feeling I was overcompulsive.
2. Disappointment at not covering the prepared material.
3. Running the danger of trying to squeeze in too much, because, after all, I have my notes in front of me.
4. Steering class time away from questions or free flowing conversation because of "3".
5. A strange feeling of dedication to my work and students, feeling that you care. Why should I be so masochistic?
6. A sense of accomplishment.
7. I might learn something from the material.
8. I will now have material for my next meeting, if it involves a continuation of the current class meeting. Thus thoughts "1" and "2" may be irrational.

BEING UNDERPREPARED

1. An intense, overwhelming, omnipresent, terrifying feeling of FEAR before and during class, "My God! What if they ask me a question which I should be prepared to answer?" Closely associated with heartpiercing guilt for having let my students down and partially wasted their time, followed by intense self-criticism for being underprepared, concluding in a firmly cemented vow, never, never, never, NEVER to let this happen again.

Morrow, R. (1976) *What every TA should know.* In *The TA at UCLA: A handbook for teaching assistants. (1977-78).* The Regents of the University of California.

HOW MUCH SHOULD YOU PREPARE IN ADVANCE?

In the beginning, many TAs feel more secure when they pre-determine the format of their classes to the last minute by arming themselves with a bale of elaborate notes containing everything from "Good morning, class, I hope you all had a good weekend," to the Farewell Address, but this kind of rigid organization has its drawbacks, the least of which is the possibility of your dropping the notes on the floor and getting all the pages in the wrong order. Constantly referring to a sheaf of notes on the desk in front of you may muffle your voice, is not conducive to your students' concentration—especially if you keep losing your place on the page—and does not exactly inspire their confidence in your abilities.

Most TAs recommend the use of no more than skeletal notes, since this allows for greater flexibility and makes it easier for you to take some initiative for discussion from the students themselves. You should, of course, study closely all the material to be dealt with in the tutorial, and attempt to anticipate the kinds of problems and questions that may arise, but student response is notoriously unreliable and even your most diligently prepared material can go unexpectedly awry. In the event of this happening you should be ready to improvise.

Woodhead, J. (1979). *A manual for teaching assistants in the department of English.* Teaching Resource Office, University of Waterloo.

BEFORE YOU WALK IN. . .

Lack of interaction may be the number one problem, but if you run a silent recitation, you can at least console yourself with the thought that it's not all your fault—the students share some of the blame—and anyway, they still probably learn something. These comforting thoughts are not available to the teachers of recitations afflicted with the number two problem: poor preparation. Listen to another unhappy undergraduate.

> **Monday morning, 10 a.m.** My recitation teacher walks into class with the homework assignment for next week. He is not sure exactly what the lecturer has covered so far, but hopes that he will be able to rely on his knowledge of the basics to get him by. He guardedly asks us if there are any questions. After a while, someone finally speaks up, asking about a point made in lecture. The instructor, not too sure of himself, gives a hand-waving, hot-air answer, which he concludes by citing the text as a reference. Another student interjects an explanation, giving examples from the lecture. Thanking the student profusely, the teacher immediately begins to work through the next assignment, using sketchy solutions he has scrawled on the back of an envelope. Every once in a while he gets stuck, and the same student has to help. Other students are talking among themselves or napping. Towards the end of the class, he remembers the graded assignments he was supposed to return; he removes the paper clip and hands the stack to a student in the front row, who passes them around. One at a time the students shuffle through the stack to find their paper, while the instructor continues to work on a problem he is having trouble with. Finally the class is over. Someone returns the unclaimed papers as the students file out.

> **Wednesday morning, 9:15 a.m.** The alarm clock rings. I roll over and reset it for 10:15.

The number two problem with recitations is that the teachers don't seem to know what they're doing—either they fumble around, or they come to class with apparently nothing special in mind and end up improvising.

What? Me unprepared? I know the subject cold.

Good, but can you explain it? That needs technique and forethought. Even if you are an experienced teacher, different lecturers have different emphases: the course may not be the same as the one you took as an undergraduate, lectured in yourself three years ago, or even taught in recitation last year.

Heine, H., Richardson, P., Mattuck, A., Taylor, E., Brown, S., Olsen, A. and Russell, C. (1986). *The torch or the firehose? A guide to section teaching*. Massachusetts Institute of Technology.

Before the Term Begins

COURSE MATERIAL

You should receive a course outline well before the term starts. Look it over to see what's emphasized and what the course aims are. Talk to the other recitation instructors, particularly those who have taught the recitations before. Get the textbook and read at least some of it for the flavor, and to judge how much explaining you'll have to do. Can the students read it by themselves?

If you are new to the course, there may be things in it you don't know so well. The earlier you start studying them the better. Later in the term when they come up you may be at a critical point in your own work and not have as much time to prepare as you would like.

STAFF MEETINGS

Before classes begin there should be a meeting with the lecturer and the other section instructors at which you can discuss the level and emphasis. In how much detail are things done, how deeply? Will old problem sets and exams be a reliable guide, or will there be changes? Administrative matters should be settled at this meeting, so that you'll have the information for your students at the first class: exams, problem sets, how it will be graded, tutorials, and so on. Sometimes the lecturer will suggest what to do the first week, to help you get started.

If the course is a new one, it may not be possible to decide everything in advance. In that case, frequent and regular course meetings during the term are essential. You should expect to give the lecturer important input on how things are going, and should expect to influence policy on exams, problem sets, and course material.

PREPARING FOR THE SECTION MEETING

Even experienced hands have to do a little thinking before each meeting, if they don't want to risk having a recitation like the one just described. At a minimum, you should have looked at the problems students are likely to ask about—make sure you can both do them and explain them. You should also know where in the syllabus the lectures have gotten, and be ready to explain what you judge to be difficult points. Talk to other instructors, read suggestion sheets put out by the lecturers, and best of all, go to the lectures yourself (this is actually required by many large courses). All these will be helpful, and let's face it, there will be days when you just don't have the time or energy for much more.

But a good section meeting demands a little more planning. Here are some things from a T.A. in physics that you might find useful:

"To prepare a presentation for the first day and indeed to map out a strategy for the entire semester, I had to decide in my own mind just what it was that I should be to the students.

"First and foremost I had to hold their attention and motivate them to succeed in learning the material.

"Once that was accomplished, I would teach them how to think about problem-solving, how to approach problems.

"Finally, I would be a person from whom the students could get additional help with course material (both in class and privately).

"Having decided that, how was I to go about realizing these objectives?

Holding Attention

"It seemed to me that providing motivation and holding their attention required two things.

"First, I had to earn their confidence since they would neither be motivated by nor interested in what I planned to say unless they could be sure that I knew what I was talking about. That meant that my part was to know the material thoroughly and prepare my presentations with a view to anticipating where possible their questions.

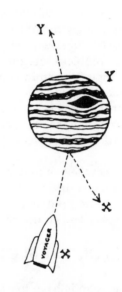

"Second, choosing problems and examples that appealed to common experience or spectacular occurrence was most likely to capture their imagination and provide motivation as well as interest. For example, working out the mechanics of the Voyager/Jupiter encounter was sure to be more interesting than just about any other momentum transfer problem. That meant that I had to look around me and think just a bit to find suitable problems—not just in text books, but all around me. (Some of the things I came up with later were: the earth as an electrical machine; the auroras; and nerve conduction.)

"Clearly preparation is important. However, a problem I had noticed in conducting tutorials was that repetition led to boredom—with each repetition, the explanation became shorter and less lucid. Therefore I decided to do many problems "off the top of my head" in class. In preparing and selecting examples I decided whether or not I saw the whole method of each problem. Those that were perfectly clear were done for the first time in front of the class, whereas those that required some more thought I worked out beforehand. In this way, I felt that an element of spontaneity was introduced which, if nothing else, allowed me to be more enthusiastic in class.

"The last element of preparation was hitting the appropriate level. Many problems can be worked out on a variety of levels. There are mathematically elegant though abstruse solutions and brute force solutions which are long but conceptually simple. I felt that this would have to be left to experience, but decided to ask some diagnostic questions the first day, to help assess the level of the students.

Thinking About Problem Solving

"The way to teach students to think about problems was, in my opinion, to emphasize in my explanations the logical method. For example, making clear what the input to a problem is, which input is physics and which is mathematics, using a diagram, and checking solutions against physical impossibilities (e.g. infinities) are all part of "method" and should be stressed.

Giving Additional Help

"As for being someone who the students might turn to for help, that only requires frequent encouragement. As I got to know the students, they felt more comfortable about seeking help from me both in class and during office hours. A good practice was to be the last one to leave the classroom, as that provided a tacit encouragement for students to come up and ask questions or indeed simply talk."

Good material, presented at the right level, and so that it teaches what you want them to learn. . . it's beginning to sound as if one could spend a whole day preparing for each section meeting. Well, things aren't that bad, though preparation does take time.

MATERIAL

Look in the textbook, perhaps at some of the non-assigned problems, and in other books; consult other section instructors and the lecturer; dredge your memory and use your imagination. Look for paradoxical results, problems where obvious reasoning leads astray, real-world problems.

LEVEL

Guess to begin with, ask other instructors, feel your way. You want something for every student––part of the time a level where everyone can follow without difficulty, part of the time a level which stretches your students just a little (nothing too complicated).

PLANNING THE HOUR

Deciding how to divide up the recitation time isn't easy. Roughly in order of priority, possible activities are: solving homework problems, reviewing the week's lectures with your own commentaries and explanations, working together on new problems, giving brief quizzes, digressing to related material not in the syllabus, telling jokes. . . Different recitations do different things.

At least do *some* advance planning—have some modest objective in mind that you can head for; it will give you an internal compass that your students will sense and appreciate. Have some alternatives in mind, if you aren't sure what your class will need that day. Do what you do best and enjoy doing, what your class seems to appreciate, what they need. Keep it varied, and keep experimenting.

Remember though to start things off with some warm-up exercises. Some teachers like to start with an outline of what went on in lecture—which can serve the same purpose, if done briefly and interactively.

BEFORE THE FIRST CLASS

CLASSROOMS

Before your first class meeting, it is wise to check the room where you will be teaching. Occasionally a clerical error occurs, causing a class to be scheduled for a broom closet or a nonexistent room number. If this happens, when you get another room, post a sign near where the assigned room would be directing students to the new location. Some difficulties can also arise regarding amount of blackboard space, number of seats, or physical condition of the classroom. If there is a problem, the room can be changed. Follow your department's policy for obtaining a room change.

During your inspection of the classroom, stand in the back of the room and determine how easy (or difficult) it is to see the blackboard. Sit in corner seats in the front and back rows to see how much of the blackboard is visible.

Humphreys, L. and Wickersham, B. (1986). *A handbook of resources for new instructors at UTK.* Learning Research Center, University of Tennessee, Knoxville.

TEXTBOOKS

By the time of your arrival on campus the textbook(s) for the course will most likely have been ordered. You will need to find out the edition, the cost and at which bookstore it may be purchased, if your college has more than one store. This is information that your students will need on the first day of class. They will appreciate knowing how much to budget for the book, and giving them the edition number prevents buying used copies of the wrong edition.

It is also a good idea to ascertain how many copies of the text were ordered. The enrollment in your class may change once the semester begins and more books may need to be ordered. Check with your department about the procedure for re-ordering books.

If there aren't enough copies of the text, not enough were ordered or if there is a problem with shipping, it is a good idea to have an alternate plan in mind. If the text is essential to the first few sessions you might consider putting library copies on reserve, placing your copy on reserve or making it available in your office, or borrowing copies from students who have already completed the course. Making copies of the text or of certain chapters is an alternative that can be considered only if it complies with departmental, university, state and federal regulations.

Some instructors also place readings on reserve at the library to be used as required or supplemental readings. Students will appreciate knowing at which library the readings are located, and the length of the time they are available for use: two hour, twenty-four hour, three day, etc. It is considered polite, if not essential, to contact the library before a specific assignment is given, so they can be prepared to have hordes of students descend upon the Reserve Desk.

Summary

Some of the points contained in this section are:

- Be prepared; it seems to be better to be over-prepared than underprepared. (p. 4)

- Skeletal notes seem to be better than elaborate, down-to-the-last-minute notes. (p. 5)

- Obtain a copy of the text and course syllabus as soon as possible and become thoroughly familiar with both. (p. 7)

- Meet with the lecturer and other section leaders to discuss the level and emphasis of the course. (p. 7)

- Be sure you can do all the problems in assigned problem sets. (p. 7)

- Attend the lectures, if you are a section leader. (p. 7)

- Prepare interesting, relevant problems and examples. (p. 8)

- Be the last to leave the classroom: it encourages the students to talk with you. (p. 9)

- Check the room before the first class to make sure it is not a broom closet. (p. 10)

- Find out the edition, cost, and purchase place of the textbook. (p. 10)

- Think of an alternate plan if not enough copies of the textbook are available. (p. 11)

- Warn the Reserve Desk at the library when a lot of students are expected. (p. 11)

2
Lecturing

The day after their discussion on preparation, Maureen and Mercedes meet Steve for lunch.

"That was good advice you gave me yesterday," says Mercedes. "I went through and prepared my first lecture for next week, and I like it."

"Good!" says Maureen. "If you like it, then chances are you'll do well when you give the lecture."

"That was my next question. How do I give a lecture? I've never done it before; I haven't really even done that much public speaking before."

"I read a poll once where people said their greatest fear was speaking in public. Death came second," contributes Steve.

"Thanks a lot, Steve. You're a big help," says Maureen.

"How do I go about making my lecture interesting? I don't want them to be bored the first day."

"What are you presenting?"

"Oh, just introductory stuff—what book we're using, getting computer accounts, when the exams are, and then an introduction to the class, talking about the topics we're going to cover. Nothing heavy."

"Sounds fine to me," says Maureen. "Look, not every lecture has to be a major extravaganza. What I've found works best is just to be yourself. Don't 'try to lecture.' Just talk to them. Only you can determine what works best. Try a couple of different things in the first few weeks and see how it feels. But don't expect it all to come at once. Give it time."

"Yeah, but how can you make Pascal programming interesting?" says Steve. "Sounds pretty dull to me."

"Really?" says Maureen. "Compared to history, I'd think anything would be exciting."

LECTURING [1]

It is a common, and often mistaken, assumption among TAs that their powers of expression are such that nobody could possibly fail to understand anything they choose to articulate. Always underestimate both your own powers of communication and your students' powers of comprehension. When you are delivering a lecture on a given subject, try to forget that you are addressing a roomful of students who may (or may not) have minds like steel traps and soaring IQs. Instead, persuade yourself that it is necessary to repeat, emphasise and re-emphasise every point of information before it will be fully grasped; you can probably remember what it was like as an undergraduate to roll into class heavy-eyed, disoriented and perhaps a bit hung over first thing in the morning.

Proceed on the premise that your students' concentration span for any one item is fifteen minutes, and that they are capable of digesting no more than four such items in any one hour.[2] When you are dealing with an item which is particularly crucial to their future academic welfare, such as The Use of the Comma, drive it home with every form of audio-visual bombardment at your disposal; emphasize it verbally, repeat it, write it on the blackboard and explain it in a handout which they can take away and peruse at their leisure.

A useful dictum is: "Tell 'em what you're going to tell 'em; tell 'em; and tell 'em what you've told 'em."[3] That is, briefly introduce what you will be talking about, if possible relating it to whatever was dealt with the week before; then explain the topic, illustrating what you say with concrete examples—preferably examples that will catch their interest by being either humourous or topical; then summarise what you have said and proceed to ask them questions which will test their understanding.

Assume that your audience is a bit deaf: speak loudly, clearly and s-l-o-w-l-y. At first, you will find that latter especially difficult, since all your instincts toward self-preservation will be urging you to hurtle through the material like an auctioneer and then fly the classroom. Another temptation, which all public speakers are told to avoid, is that of addressing yourself to the most sympathetic members of your audience, which may well be your feet. Try to make eye contact with every student in the room at some point in the course of a lecture.

Bear in mind that you are not an automaton, and neither are your students. Don't talk *at* them; try rather to talk *with* them. They have not come just to listen to your Grand Orations any more than you have come to deliver them. They are more likely to benefit by participating actively in the learning process than just sitting there passively listening to you. Getting your students involved in this way is not, however, always as easy in practice as it sounds in theory.

Woodhead, J. (1979). *A manual for teaching assistants in the department of English.* Teaching Resource Office, University of Waterloo.

[1]As a matter of interest, and to most TAs it is no more than a matter of interest, some professors give their TAs the opportunity of taking their place in the lecture hall and giving The Big Lecture. Few TAs volunteer to undergo this ordeal in sheer terror, but one TA who was man enough to try it, claimed that it was a "very worthwhile experience."

[2]These statistics, and some of the advice that follows, were obtained from *How To Succeed As A New Teacher: A Handbook for Teaching Assistants* (New Rochelle: Change Magazine Press, 1978).

[3]*How To Succeed As a New Teacher.*

LECTURING

Eble (1976) considers that "The best general advice to the teacher who would lecture is still 'Don't lecture.' That is, for most of teaching, to think in terms of discourse—talk, conversation––rather than lecture." Discussion, recitation, labs, demonstrations, problem solving, combined with lectures, offer excellent variety in a course.

Lecturing is often viewed as "the easy way out," while in actuality, lecturing *well* is perhaps the most difficult method of presenting facts, since it takes an inordinate amount of preparation time and energy. Soliciting information from students takes class time. For this reason, when a substantial volume of vital information needs to be transmitted to students quickly, lecturing sometimes appears inevitable.

Instructors have the responsibility of presenting good, accurate, substantial lectures and to do that with enthusiasm and interest. Students expect to hear "the truth" and to learn something. They also hope to enjoy the process. No small bill to fill!

The following article on lecturing, reprinted from the *Chronicle of Higher Education* gives some useful suggestions on lecturing. Some of the ideas listed below come from *How to Succeed as a New Teacher*, Change Magazine Press, 1978, while others were suggested in *Teaching Assistance: A Handbook of Teaching Ideas*, from The University of California at San Diego.

- Break a lecture every few minutes with an exercise that involves students actively. Rhetorical questions, anecdotes, problems, and the act of relating ideas to current events all interrupt the thrust of the lecture but give the student's mind an "exercise break."

- Make eye contact with each student at least once during the lecture. This personalizes the lecture and increases a student's sense of involvement.

- Do not read a lecture. Using a set of guide notes to make certain you cover all intended items and to contain details not worth memorizing, however, is quite reasonable. The lecturer must think continually about and plan the next few sentences of the topic, whereas the reader simply reads, thereby boring students.

- Give students a "road map" at the start of the class, put an outline on the blackboard. This helps students organize your material and recognize major transition points.

- Conclude each lecture. Bring the lecture to some logical culmination: summarize, restate key points, relate a major portion to a practical example, or make the students use the material you have just covered to test their understanding. Do not make it seem as if the clock forced you to stop at some arbitrary point.

- Do not be bound by the 50-minute rule. Not all material can be neatly segmented into 50-minute blocks. If you have completed one major topic in 40 minutes and the next one is likely to require another 20 minutes, it may be better to pause and answer questions, relate the day's material to current events, discuss an assigned class project, comment on questions appropriate for the next exam, or dismiss the students early.

Humphreys, L. and Wickersham, B. (1976). *A handbook of resources for new instructors at UTK.* Learning Research Center, University of Tennessee, Knoxville.

- Do not run more than a couple of minutes over the end of the period. Students may have other classes some distance away or other appointments.

- When appropriate, allow students to influence the direction of the class by suggesting topics they would like to have presented.

THE ART OF LECTURING:
A FEW SIMPLE IDEAS CAN HELP TEACHERS IMPROVE THEIR SKILLS

Ask corporate executives which of their skills need sharpening and they're likely to mention public speaking, says Jerry Tarver, professor of speech communication at the University of Richmond. College teachers, on the other hand, whose success in the classroom may well depend on their ability to communicate orally, seem far less interested in that kind of self-improvement, he says.

Many colleges and universities, moreover, do little to help faculty members refine skills—such as speaking and lecturing—that would make them better teachers, says William E. Cashin, an educational-development specialist at Kansas State University's Center for Faculty Evaluation and Development in Higher Education.

But according to specialists in speech and faculty development, faculty members can use a few simple ideas and techniques to become better lecturers and instructors.

KNOWING WHAT ACTORS DO

"You don't have to be a frustrated actor or ham to be a good teacher, but you do have to know how to control your voice, emotions, and body as actors do," says David N. Tobin, a former assistant professor of humanities at Emory University who is now an account representative and speechwriter at the Houston office of Ogilvy & Mather Public Relations.

Because doctoral programs generally emphasize research abilities but ignore lecturing skills, Mr. Cashin says, new Ph.D.'s often experience a sense of "cognitive dissonance" when they start teaching. They find, he says, that "the thing they do most is what they are least prepared to do."

A young instructor at one Midwestern college says many teachers are too proud to admit that their lecturing skills need improvement. But this teacher, believing she would have to work especially hard to prove her competence in a field dominated by men, says she sought the help of a faculty-development specialist to build up her confidence in lecturing to large groups.

They used videotapes of her lectures to identify her strong points, she says, and minimize "the things that are irritating," such as her tendency to raise her voice at the end of sentences.

The instructor also asked colleagues and friends—people with various interests and knowledge of her field—to analyze her lectures and material she handed out to students. She says the fact that they had different perspectives was especially helpful.

Lawrence M. Aleamoni, Director of Instructional Research and Development at the University of Arizona, says young teachers often make the mistake of imitating teaching styles they found satisfying as students. They end up with forced presentations, he says, and fail to develop their own style.

Palmer, S. (1983). The art of lecturing: A few simple ideas can help teachers improve their skills. *Chronicle of Higher Education*, April 13, p. 19.

"If your personality and style don't fit with the one you're trying to mimic, then you're doing a tremendous disservice to the students," Mr. Aleamoni says.

Mr. Cashin says that instructors who rely mainly on their personal learning experiences as a guide to lecturing often find that their efforts backfire. They should realize, he says, that "all students do not necessarily learn the way you do."

Instead, he says, faculty members should observe other teachers and analyze why they are effective: How do they organize their lectures, for example, and how much attention do they pay to students' responses?

OTHER SUGGESTIONS

Speech and faculty-development specialists make these other suggestions for improving classroom presentations:

Determine the Specific Objectives of the Lecture
Ask yourself what you want students to remember about the lecture next week, says Nancy A. Diamond, education specialist in the Office of Instructional Resources at the University of Illinois at Urbana. Then decide what they should still remember next year.

But keep in mind that "straight" lectures may not be the best approach, says Bette L. Erikson, instructional-development specialist at the University of Rhode Island. Depending on their goals, she says, teachers should consider whether informal discussions, for example, might be more appropriate for certain material.

Find Out What Students Already Know—and What They Want to Know
Analyze their needs and interests at the beginning of a course to guide your choice of material and approach.

Outline Goals for Each Lecture
Use the blackboard, written instructions, and inflections of voice to let students know which elements of the lecture you consider to be most important.

Relate Lecture Themes to the Course As a Whole
Emphasize the relationship between what you are teaching now and what you taught last week.

Illustrate Points Frequently
One example is not enough for most students, says Ms. Erikson. She adds that the best examples are those that draw on students' experiences, so instructors should try to keep up with the latest campus events and trends.

Deliver the Lecture Extemporaneously
Use notes as a guide to talking about a subject, but don't read them to the class. "You can read without thinking, but you can't talk without thinking," says Mr. Tarver, adding that an extemporaneous delivery makes the presentation more natural and conversational. Such lectures may not be perfectly "fluent," he says, but they help keep students attentive.

Point Out Transitions Between Concepts

As an aid to students, Mr. Tarver suggests, instructors should actually number the major themes of their lectures, summarize concepts, and ask questions about each element.

Adjust Lecture Style to Students' Attention Span

They generally start to lose their capacity to concentrate about 15 to 20 minutes into a lecture, says W. J. McKeachie, professor of psychology and Director of the Center for Research on Learning and Teaching at the University of Michigan.

He recommends that faculty members break up their lectures by using the blackboard and audiovisual materials, asking questions, giving students a problem to solve, or taking a short break.

Make Sure Questions-and-Answer Sessions Are Carefully Planned

While questions can provide an effective change of pace, well-designed questions can also have many other benefits, notes Ms. Diamond of the University of Illinois. But asking a simple "yes-or-no" question—or merely asking, "Any questions?"—is not likely to work well, she says. Instead, instructors can give students specific clues about the kind of answers expected of them.

For example, says Ms. Diamond, ask something like, "What generalizations can you make about the topic we've been discussing?"

Students are more likely to participate when they are confident that the lecturer will work out the answers to questions with them, says LuAnn Wilkerson, Director of Faculty Development at the Medical College of the University of Wisconsin at Milwaukee.

She says many faculty members intimidate students by moving away from those who give incorrect answers. Better, she says, is to work toward the solution with those who don't have the right answers.

Ms. Diamond adds that teachers also need to be ready to rephrase questions until students are comfortable enough to respond.

Because students are often unwilling to answer questions in front of large groups, Mr. Cashin of Kansas State recommends asking them to hold up color-coded charts indicating their answers to a series of questions. Students will take a more active role this way, and instructors can gauge how well the entire class is picking up the material.

Show Students You Want Them to Ask Questions

They may assume, mistakenly, that a rapid-fire speaker is purposely moving quickly to avoid questions. To dispel that notion, be sure to take long pauses, so students will have a chance to formulate questions. Instructors also can demonstrate an openness to questions by moving toward the audience and maintaining eye contact with the students during the lecture. Repetitive questions can be discouraged, meanwhile, if answers are written on the blackboard as they come up.

Regularly Evaluate Your Effectiveness

Faculty members need to know which lecturing techniques are working well for them—and which are not. Robert J. Menges, Program Director at Northwestern University's Center for Teaching and the Professions, suggests surveying the whole class by asking students to write answers to one or two questions, such as "What was the most stimulating part of today's lecture?" or "I was most confused when . . ."

Invite Colleagues in Other Fields to Evaluate Your Lectures

Getting advice from faculty members who are not familiar with the jargon and research of your discipline can help you make your lectures more comprehensible. Members of your own department can help with content-related questions, of course, but are less likely to focus on your actual lecture style, notes Robert M. Diamond, Assistant Vice-Chancellor and Director of the Center for Instructional Development at Syracuse University.

Study the Performing Arts

Teachers have more in common with actors than they often acknowledge, says Mr. Tobin of Ogilvy & Mather. "They face the same dilemma of having to repeat the same material over and over again: How do you make it new?" he says. By studying actors' techniques for controlling their voices and movements, teachers can become more conscious of ways they can control—and improve—their own speaking ability.

Scrutinize Your Own Behavior in Small-Group Situations

While most faculty members have little trouble speaking to a few students or colleagues, many of them don't effectively transfer their speaking abilities to larger groups, says Mr. Tarver. Determine your strengths in less-threatening settings and use those assets to improve your lecturing style.

Also note how you use nonverbal communication in a small group, advises Mr. McKeachie, as a guide to lecturing before a large class.

Concentrate on Enhancing One Skill at a Time

According to speech experts, lecturers seeking to improve are more likely to do so gradually than all at once. If they are working on improved eye contact with students, for instance, they should not try to change radically other aspects of their delivery at the same time, the experts say.

And if a new technique flops, says Mr. Aleamoni of the University of Arizona, it's best to admit mistakes openly to the class. Teachers who do so will still be able to maintain an air of professionalism, he says. They also may gain respect from students by showing that they are not afraid to take risks or concede failure.

ADVANTAGES AND DISADVANTAGES OF THE LECTURE METHOD

Advantages

The "good" lecture

- permits dissemination of unpublished or not readily available material.

- allows the instructor to precisely determine the aims, content, organization, pace and direction of a presentation. In contrast, more student-centered methods, e.g., discussions or laboratories, require the instructor to deal with unanticipated student ideas, questions and comments.

- can be used to arouse interest in a subject.

- can complement and clarify text material.

- complements certain individual learning preferences. Some students depend upon the structure provided by highly teacher-centered methods.

- facilitates large class communication.

Disadvantages

However, the lecture also

- places students in a passive rather than an active role. Passivity hinders learning.

- encourages one-way communication; therefore, the lecturer must make a conscious effort to become aware of student problems and student understanding of content.

- requires a considerable amount of unguided student time outside of the classroom to enable understanding and long-term retention of content. In contrast, interactive methods (discussion, problem-solving sessions) allow the instructor to influence students when they are actively working with the material.

- requires the instructor to have or to learn effective writing, speaking and modeling skills.

Diamond, N., Sharp, G. and Ory, J. *Improving your lecturing.* Office of Instructional Resources, University of Illinois at Urbana Champaign.

SUGGESTIONS FOR EFFECTIVE LECTURE PREPARATION AND DELIVERY

Lecturing refers to both planning and delivering a classroom presentation rather than a formal speech. While both oral presentations have certain elements in common, a classroom lecture places greater emphasis on the importance of presenter-audience (instructor-student) interaction. Following is a brief listing of suggestions for effective lecture preparation and delivery. The suggestions are arranged under one of the three phases of a lecture—the introduction, the body and the closing.

At the Beginning of the Lecture

A.   Plan an introduction to catch the listener's interest.

Suggestion: Raise a question to be answered by the end of the lecture.

Example: *"By the end of the hour, you should be able to answer the question, 'Are essay test questions better than objective test questions?'"*

Suggestion: State an historical or current problem related to the lecture content.

Example: *"It was conjectured by Gauss that the number of primes up to any point x was less than a certain smooth easily calculated function of x. This conjecture was supported by extensive numerical evidence. However, in 1914, Littlewood proved that, in fact, the relation becomes false for an infinite sequence of large x's. Let's take a look at Littlewood's reasoning."*

Suggestion: Explain the relationship of lecture content to laboratory exercises, homework problems, professional career interests, etc.

Example: *"Today, I'll lecture on cost of living indices, a topic in macroeconomics which will help you understand the recent discussions in Congress related to inflation."*

Suggestion: Relate lecture content to previous class material.

Example: *"For the past few weeks, Skinner, Osgood and others who take a behaviorist view of language acquisition have occupied our attention. Today, I'll introduce another different perspective on language acquisition and learning. We'll spend the rest of this week and the next on understanding this view and comparing it with the behaviorist position."*

B.   Provide a brief general overview of the lecture's content.

Example: *"In Victorian England the conflict between religion and science was well reflected in the literature of the time. Today we'll look at two poems 'In Memorium,' and 'Dover Beach,' which illustrate this conflict."*

C.   Tell students how you expect them to use the lecture material.

Example: *"Today I'll offer a specific model of evaluation and illustrate its applicability in several kinds of settings. When you meet in your discussion groups this week, you'll be asked to apply the model as you discuss* Brown vs. the Board of Education *decision."*

D.   Define or explain unfamiliar terminology.

Example: *"In physics, the term* work *has a precise technical meaning. The work done by a force F when the object on which it acts moves a distance Δs (puts a drawing on the board) is defined by $\Delta W = F_s \Delta s$ denotes the work. It is assumed that F does not change much during the motion through the distance Δs. F_s denotes the component of F in the direction of the motion and can be positive, zero or negative. Now let's look at this diagram and see how well you understand the definition of work."*

During the Body of the Lecture

ORGANIZATION

A.   Allow for some flexibility in the presentation in order to respond to student questions and comments.

B.   Determine which key points can be effectively developed during the class session. It is necessary to strike a balance between depth and breadth of coverage. When every nuance, detail or instance of a topic is discussed students often lose sight of the main ideas. Or, when too many ideas are presented and not developed, students fail to gain understanding.

C.   Organize material in some logical order. Suggested organizational schemes include:

Cause-Effect
Events are cited and explained by reference to their origins. For example, one can demonstrate how the continental revolutionary movements of the late 1700s affected British politics at the turn of the century.

Time Sequential
Lecture ideas are arranged chronologically. For example, a lecturer explaining the steps in a clinical supervision model, talks about the first step to be undertaken, the second step, and so forth.

Topical

Parallel elements of different discussion topics are focused on successively. For example, a professor lecturing about the differential features of common diseases in canines and felines speaks about their etiologies, typical histories, predisposing factors, etc.

Problem-Solution

The statement of a problem is followed by alternate solutions. For example, a lecture on the Cuban missile crisis may begin with a statement of the foreign policy problem followed by a presentation of the alternative solution available to President Kennedy.

Pro-Con

A two-sided discussion of a given topic is presented. For example, a lecture is organized around the advantages and disadvantages of using the lecture method of instruction.

Ascending-Descending

Lecture topics are arranged according to their importance, familiarity or complexity. For example, in a lecture introducing students to animal diseases, the diseases of primary importance may be discussed first, followed by discussion of diseases of secondary importance and concluding with coverage of the diseases of tertiary importance.

D.   Allow time within the lecture to summarize key ideas.

E.   Prepare relevant examples to illustrate key ideas.

F.   Provide transitions which show the relationships between key ideas.

G.   Throughout the lecture check on student understanding by:

    1.   Asking students to answer specific questions.

        Example: *"Okay now, who can describe in his/her own words the theory of neuron transmission?"*

    2.   Asking for student questions.

        Example: *"Did you have any questions about the application of Kirchoff's rules in problem 6?"*

    3.   Presenting a problem or situation which requires use of lecture material in order to obtain a solution.

        Example: *"Over the last few days we have been discussing regression analysis. How can we use this information to predict your final grade in this course when given your mid-term scores and the correlation between mid-term and final scores?"*

    4.   Watching the class for nonverbal cues of confusion or misunderstanding.

        Example: *Look for loss of eye contact, talking, clock watching, etc.*

Closing the Lecture

A. Answer any questions raised at the beginning of the lecture.

B. Provide closure for the lecture. Suggestions include:

    1. Briefly summarize lecture material and preview what lies ahead.

        Example: *"Today I have identified five phases of the reflective thinking process. Tomorrow we will see how these phases can be useful for our understanding of human learning."*

    2. Relate lecture material to past or future presentations.

        Example: *"During the next lesson, we'll break into discussion groups and get some experience applying the evaluation model discussed in class today to the first three case studies in your file."*

    3. Ask a student to summarize the lecture's key ideas.

        Example: *"Who will summarize the key issues developed during today's lecture?"*

C. Restate what you expect the students to gain from the lecture material.

        Example: *"As I stated in the introduction, given the appropriate data you should be able to plot the appropriate supply and demand curves."*

D. Ask for and answer student questions.

The Following Questions Relating to Lecture Delivery Should Be Considered Throughout All Three Phases of Lecturing:

DELIVERY—VOCAL

Do you:

1. cue important ideas by varying speech rate, volume and pitch?

2. speak to students and not to the blackboard, walls, notes or floor?

3. enunciate clearly?

4. let your sense of humor show?

5. avoid repetition of pet words or phrases (e.g., okay, uh)?

DELIVERY—PHYSICAL

Do you:

1. establish and maintain eye contact with your students?

2. use gestures and physical movements which complement your verbal statements (e.g., looking at students while asking for student questions)?

3. practice in advance with audio-visuals?

4. avoid using distracting gestures or physical movements (e.g., grooming, pacing)?

EFFECTIVE TEACHING TECHNIQUES

Lecturing

OBJECTIVES

At the end of the presentation each participant should be able to name four instructional behaviors which correlate positively with student achievement and describe several specific techniques.

1. Stimulus statement: "There are no dull subjects, only dull teachers and dull teaching methods.

2. Purpose of lecturing:
   a. To inspire, motivate, maintain attention;
   b. To transfer information from instructor to student;
   c. To provide a structure for organizing and remembering information; and
   d. To point out sources for further related information.

3. Instructor behaviors which seem to correlate positively with student achievement:
   a. Acting in a businesslike manner;
   b. Giving clear and well-organized presentations that include introductory and concluding statements;
   c. Providing a variety of teaching styles, course materials, and class activities, and;
   d. Displaying enthusiasm (by eye contact, gesturing, dynamic delivery).

4. Lecturing can be enhanced by:
   a. Telling students what will happen;
   b. Providing a map or structure of the territory;
   c. Requiring student responses;
   d. Using attention-getting devices;
   e. Using redundant information stimuli; and
   f. Explaining reasons for assignments; criteria to be used in evaluation.

REFERENCES

Costin, F. (1972). "Lecturing versus other methods of teaching; A review of research." *British Journal of Educational Technology*, vol. 3, no 1.

Hall, W.C. & Curran, A. (1975). *University Teaching*, Advisory Committee for University Education, University of Adelaide, pp. 31-40.

McKeachie, W.J. (1969). *Teaching Tips*, 6th edition. New York: D.C. Heath & Co., pp. 22-36.

McLeish, J. (1968). *The Lecture Method*. Cambridge Institute of Education, pp. 60.

Ely, D. (1987). *Effective teaching techniques: lecturing.* Presentation at the Seminar on Teaching, Syracuse University, February.

Summary

Some of the points contained in this section are:

- Underestimate your powers of explanation and your students powers of comprehension. (p. 14)

- Plan as if your students' attention span is 15 minutes for one item. (pp. 14, 19)

- Tell them what you're going to tell them, tell them, then tell them what you told them. (p. 14)

- Talk slowly. (p. 14)

- Make eye contact with everyone. (pp. 14, 26)

- Talk *with* the students, not at them. (p. 14)

- Break a lecture every few minutes. (p. 15)

- If you can, don't lecture at all. (p. 15)

- Do not read a lecture. (pp. 15, 18, 19)

- Put up an outline of the class. (pp. 15, 18)

- Allow time to summarize key ideas and to conclude each lecture. (pp. 15, 23, 24)

- Do not be bound by the 50-minute rule. (p. 15)

- Do not run over class time. (p. 16)

- If appropriate, allow students to suggest class topics. (p. 16)

- Observe other teachers and analyze their effectiveness. (p. 18)

- Determine the specific objectives of the course. (p. 18)

- Find out what students already know and what they want to know. (p. 18)

- Relate lecture themes to the course as a whole. (pp. 18, 22)

- Illustrate points frequently. (p. 18)

- Point out transitions between concepts. (p. 19)

- Carefully plan question-answer sessions. (p. 19)

- Show students you want them to ask questions. (p. 19)

- Regularly evaluate your effectiveness. (p. 19)

- Invite colleagues in other fields to evaluate your lectures. (p. 20)

- Study the performing arts. (p. 20)

- Scrutinize your own behavior in small-group situations. (p. 20)

- Concentrate on enhancing one skill at a time. (p. 20)

- Plan an introduction to catch the listener's attention. (p. 22)

- Tell students how you expect them to use the lecture material. (pp. 23, 25)

- Define or explain unfamiliar terminology. (p. 23)

- Check on student understanding throughout the lecture. (p. 24)

- Cue important ideas by varying speech rate, volume, and pitch. (p. 26)

- Avoid using distracting gestures. (p. 26)

- Act in a business-like manner. (p. 27)

- Display enthusiasm. (p. 27)

3
Discussion

Maureen and Mercedes are sitting in the Graduate Center lounge when Steve walks in.

"Hi gang! Where are you watching the game on Saturday?"

They don't even look up. They are poring over the new class schedule for the next semester.

Steve slams his book on the table and yells, "That's it, that's the final straw! First my discussion class ignores my questions and now you two ignore me. I've had it!"

Mercedes and Maureen look up annoyed, but soften when they see a look of real concern and worry on his face.

"Calm down, Steve. Tell us all about it," says Mercedes.

"Thanks," sighs Steve as he slumps into a chair.

"Well, I didn't want to admit it before, but things do not bode well in my discussion class. They just won't talk. They'll answer my questions in as few words as possible, and that's it, which is bad. There are a lot of issues that we cover in this course that just don't have any one answer. One of the purposes of the course is to get the students to think about all the different sides to these issues and the reasons behind some of the decisions that shaped history. I thought that there was some very fertile ground for interesting discussions in this class, but today, in the first session, zip."

"That is a problem," Maureen agrees. "What have you tried?"

"Everything! I've asked all kinds of questions, I've waited for answers, I've asked for people to expand on their answers, I've asked if there was any agreement or disagreement with any of the answers given and all I get is nodding heads!"

"Maybe the students are shy or unprepared," suggests Mercedes.

"Maybe," admits Steve, "but it's a *discussion* group and they're supposed to *discuss!*"

"Why don't you give them a question to think about ahead of time? That way they can prepare, do the reading, and think of an answer," says Maureen.

"It's worth a try. I just thought of something else. Since lots of these issues have at least two sides to them, I could divide the class up and give each group a side of the issue. Then they could prepare and each group could present their side of the story at the next class," Steve says, excited.

"Not bad, Steve," says Mercedes. "Working in groups may lessen the fear of some of the shy students."

"Do you feel better now?" asks Maureen.

"Yeah, I do. Thanks. You guys come in handy every now and again. Let's go eat."

"He's talking food again," says Maureen. "He must feel better."

DISCUSSIONS

One of the most common TAing activities is leading discussions. I learned from evaluations that the students expect the TA to lead the discussions. They don't want other students bullshitting. They want to discuss the central issues of the class.

Discussions differ from lectures in many ways. A couple are that the students can be more active and that there can be more personal contact. Decide what kind of discussion is most useful for your class. Is there a certain topic to be discussed? Does the group have to reach a conclusion or come to agreement? Is there a subject matter that must be learned? Is it a forum for expressing and comparing views? Is it important that the students carefully analyze the topic or that they learn such skills? (If your group is one which needs to learn material and come to conclusions about it, *Learning Thru Discussion* by William Fawcett Hill can be a very useful book.)

Once you have decided what kind of discussion you want, tell the students. If you don't they will just try to psych you out anyway. It's important to pay attention to the kinds of questions you ask and how you ask them. The students will answer the questions at the level you ask them. If you want them to respond with deliberated thought you have to give them enough time to think and answer. The three seconds it takes can seem like an eternity, but once the students start responding the value of waiting becomes apparent.

After you begin carefully choosing the level of your questions (and comments) and giving the students time to think, you will find that your participation in the discussion diminishes. Your functions will then be to monitor the discussion and, when necessary, redirect it. It may be useful to summarize the course of the discussion periodically in order to focus student attention or reinforce key points. With mature students you may not even have to participate. With other groups you may find that you are constantly redirecting the discussion.

Among the problems TAs face in leading discussions are that the students may not be prepared for the topic the TA wants to discuss, and that the students do not have enough in common to get a broad-based conversation going. One way to give coherence to discussions is to assign specific tasks ahead of time. The entire class can be given a specific assignment, or selected students can be given special assignments. Another technique which usually leads to lively discussions is to divide the class into groups and have two groups prepare arguments on opposite sides of an issue. Each side then presents its case to the rest of the class, and responds to the other side's arguments. Breaking the class into small groups owes part of its effect to the fact that it gives the individual students a personal stake in the classroom action. Students generally respond when given personal responsibility.

For my first TAing experience, I had to lead discussions in a political philosophy class. Since I had only one such course myself—and that had been eight years earlier—I was a bit apprehensive about the assignment. I decided to let the students discuss whatever they wanted as long as it encouraged understanding and analysis. Somebody spoke up right away.

(That was nice—no long pause.) Another person responded on a different topic. (Oh, no! What should I do?) The third student went back to the first topic. (Some relief.) Soon the two topics merged. (Such luck!)

Morrow, R. (1976). *What every TA should know.* In *The TA at UCLA: A handbook for teaching assistants. (1977-78).* The Regents of the University of California.

In this case the students themselves controlled the discussion. I soon learned which ones to call on to keep it from straying. If they take the responsibility, let them and count it a blessing: don't force your role. Otherwise assert your control firmly, gently and supportively. I also suggest some patience. Don't think you have to fill in every pause. Look around for someone who is obviously thinking, who might want to speak out but seems hesitant, and ask if that person has something to add. If you ask deep questions and pause pensively, you might encourage thinking. If the students know that considered thought is what you expect, their natural tendency is to respond to those expectations.

USING CLASS DISCUSSION
AS A TEACHING TOOL

WHAT IS CLASS DISCUSSION?

Periods of classtime during which the faculty member or a discussion leader guides student discussion of specific course content for learning purposes.

WHY USE IT?

Active participation in good discussion is stimulating, bringing greater ego-involvement in the subject matter through the process. It gives the instructor an opportunity to check student understandings and to note, and sometimes change, their attitudes towards specific content. It can add variety and change-of-pace to the semester.

WHEN TO USE IT?

It is just one teaching tool and therefore need not totally substitute for any other such as lecturing. It is best used after the class has a common knowledge base on a specific area gained through reading and research. It is best for subject matter which involves application, analysis, synthesis, and interpretations of material rather than collections of facts. It is vital to the "Case Method" and many graduate seminars.

HOW DOES THE INSTRUCTOR PREPARE?

In the previous class, talk about student role and preparation. The discussion topic should be roughly outlined and divided into major sub-heads with 3-4 key study questions framed for each section with approximate timing to be used for each section. Students should get this ahead of time.

HOW DO STUDENTS PREPARE?

With common readings, specific research on segments, study of outline given.

HOW TO ARRANGE THE ROOM?

Discussion takes place most effectively when students can be face-to-face, rather than in lecture-style seating. Approximations of a circle provides the best facilitation for participation.

HOW SHOULD THE DISCUSSION BE LED?

Faculty need to understand the neutral-guidance-questioner role of the leader as a facilitator. Care must be taken that lengthy lectures are not given by the faculty member because only brief factual inputs may be needed. Restraint and patience are required rather than domination.

Funk, F. (1987). *Using class discussion as a teaching tool.* Presentation at the Seminar on Teaching, Syracuse University, February.

The leader should:

1. Introduce the topic and its importance, briefly.

2. Mention sub-areas to be covered and timing for each.

3. Give simple ground rules: each should speak up without being called upon, address each other.

4. Get discussion started with a prepared first question: short, stimulating, easy to have an opinion about. *Wait it out*—someone will pick it up.

5. Guide group thinking, impartially and without talking too much yourself, by using questions as your guidance tool to probe, challenge, rephrase their comments. (For question types, see *Chronicle*, 7-25-84)

6. Summarize what has been said periodically then redirect the group to the next topic sub-area with a new question.

7. Be generally accepting; don't constantly make evaluative comments that punish and reward, rather ask examining questions.

8. Encourage general participation by using questions such as: "How do the rest of you feel about this?" or "Are there other reactions?"

9. Keep the discussion "on track". If it seems to be on a tangent, ask the group about the connection to the subject.

10. Listen carefully and ask impromptu probing questions which make the students examine their views carefully, cite evidence for views, examine assumptions, and raise the abstraction level.

HOW SHOULD IT BE ENDED?

1. Allow time at the end for a summary by the leader or the group. Invite the group's agreement on the summary.

2. Give the class a feeling of accomplishment by suggesting that it was a fruitful exchange of important ideas.

3. Suggest next steps or assignment to follow-up.

4. Evaluate results after class for issues ignored or key questions only partially considered.

GENERAL COMMENTS

Good classroom discussion is not a bull-session exchange of ignorance where students just talk in an undirected way and the faculty member just listens. Sloppy thinking, lack of facts or unexamined opinions are not good discussion. On the other hand, a kind of "fishing-game" discussion is also not appropriate. This is where the faculty member conducts discussion (really recitations) until a student stumbles on the "right" or faculty answer.

CLASS PARTICIPATION

For all classes led by TAs, the issue of class participation, or the lack of it, may represent a minor crisis. If your class seems unwilling to communicate, try any or all of the following.

Scrutinize your attitude towards your class. Are you open, friendly and honest? Your own inspiration with, and interest in, any particular topic will do much to break the ice. Try asking a series of questions that you consider answerable immediately, but sufficiently above the common sense level to let the class know that it is not their basic intelligence you are questioning. Avoid general questions directed to the class as a whole. Use varying approaches in your questioning. Ask for and give concrete examples. Ask one of the class members directly, but avoid making the student feel silly if he or she cannot answer. If the session involves more questioning than true discussion, the manner in which you respond to the first replies is very important. Encourage any answer, gradually turning the answers towards the real issues. Once the first question has been answered, the session will probably go more smoothly. Do not be afraid of silences. Give the students time to think about answers. A 20 second silence feels like an hour, but may be more valuable than idle chatter. Use the blackboard for drawing diagrams and illustrating ideas. Encourage the students to write their ideas down on paper and then call on several to read them out. This approach puts the students less on-the-spot than direct questioning as they have time to plan their answer, and can now read it out.

If the class is of the seminar type where discussion is likely to be protracted, start discussion somewhere near the subject area. Then sit back and be quiet. Endless chatter on your part is not a good way to promote discussion. Listen carefully and when discussion tends to be irrelevant to the main focus, gently direct, by suggestions and questions, its course back to the subject of the day. If an impasse is reached or the topic is exhausted, be prepared to summarize and give your own opinion. Students expect that you will round off a discussion and resolve problems as necessary, so do your best to offer reassurance. Don't be surprised if the students who say the least in class do the best in written tests. It just seems to work that way sometimes.

An alternate means by which discussion of a particular topic could be approached is to divide the class into a number of subgroups (3 is a good number) and ask them to consider the questions. Present both the format for discussion and the question itself in such a way that it is not perceived as an ultimatum, but is merely an alternative approach. During this discussion, move between groups and, if necessary, offer suggestions. Give the students 5-10 minutes for group discussion and then call on one person from each group to summarize the group's thoughts.

If you are instructing one of the physical courses, the format may be considerably different. Introduction of the lab may provide an opportunity for discussion, but the balance of the session is set aside for the students to work on the lab, with your guidance. One approach may be to encourage group participation, but individual write-ups. The students will feel more comfortable in talking to you and asking questions if you are casually walking around the class instead of sitting behind a desk at the front of the room.

Cotton, A. (1979). *Guidelines for teaching assistants in Geography.* Geography Department, Teaching Resource Office, University of Waterloo.

THE GLASS WALL:
ENCOURAGING INTERACTION

The number one problem in teaching recitations is the "glass wall"—the teacher on one side doing a passable job of explaining, talking, and writing, but rarely interacting with the students on the other side. Listen to an undergraduate describe it.

> We're usually all there when he walks in. He looks sort of embarrassed, stares down at his desk and asks if we have any questions. There's an awkward silence, like at a party where nobody can think of anything to say. Then he starts to work a problem from the homework. He talks to the blackboard in a steady even way. You can hear, but you can't tell what's important and what isn't. I can't follow one of the steps, but I'm afraid to say anything. Every now and then he says, O.K.?, but it doesn't mean anything and he doesn't stop. After a while you don't really understand much and wonder why you're there. I copy the stuff into my notebook—I'll probably be able to figure it out at home— but if it weren't for the exam I know I'd never look at it.
>
> I guess I keep going because I know that otherwise I'd just waste the hour some other way. He knows his stuff all right, but it's like he's up front and we're back there and there's a glass wall between us.

A recitation without interaction—what problem could be more basic? Without the ease of communication that's supposed to be fostered by small groups, why have recitations at all?

The silence is bad for you: it makes it hard for you to know the difficulties your students are having. You can't tell if your explanation is opening the door, or whether you need to try another key in the lock.

It's bad for your students, who already have sat through many lectures and don't really want another one from you. They need a chance to talk and express themselves, to clarify their own thinking, to share their difficulties with each other, to experience the feeling of a group

Heine, H., Richardson, P., Mattuck, A., Taylor, E., Brown, S., Olsen, A. and Russell C. (1986). *The torch or the firehose? A guide to section teaching.* Massachusetts Institute of Technology.

working together on mutual problems. This is what recitations are about, and getting it to happen in yours ought to be your number one priority.

Breaking Down the Glass Wall

Achieving real communication with your students isn't always easy. Think of all the situations in ordinary life where two people find communication difficult; add to them the extra complications that arise when one of them is an authority figure, and the other must talk with an audience of peers listening. You're going to need some tact and skill; here are some suggestions.

GET THEM THINKING: ASK QUESTIONS

Your students have just arrived and are sitting there thinking about life's problems, about the class they just came from, or maybe about nothing at all.

"Any questions?"

Questions? They can't even remember what the current topic is in your course. They thumb through their notebooks, but it's hard to start out cold.

Your first task is to get their mental sap flowing. Ask some easy review questions (very easy, if you suspect they are far behind). If you are handing back a problem set, give them a typical mistake and ask what the error is. You could give them a few minutes to work by themselves or in small groups on an easy problem you give out, maybe cast as an informal quick quiz. This can be done in the middle of the period too, to break up the class hour. You'll see how much livelier things will become when everyone has thought about the same problem.

When you start on new material, try to cast it in the form of a problem to be solved, and have them think about it for a bit. Ask for suggestions and deal with them seriously: don't just dismiss all the ideas which ultimately won't work, or it will be the last time you'll get any response.

In preparing, look for paradoxes that you can spring on your students, and be rewarded by the sight of them sitting forward in their seats thinking. Actually, they will do the same thing if you've made a mistake you can't find right away, and some wily teachers have been known to make mistakes on purpose for that reason.

PEER-GROUP PRESSURE

If things still seem sticky—you are asking good questions, but get only nervous looks in return—your students are probably afraid of saying something that will make them look foolish in front of the others. Sometimes you will see students silently mouthing an answer they don't dare to say aloud.

Perhaps you have felt this way yourself in advanced courses or seminars. If so, you will appreciate that it is a difficult problem to deal with. The ultimate solution has to be for them to feel comfortable with each other, but this won't happen right away. Meanwhile you can help a lot by being supportive: "That's a good question, Jennifer" or "I'll bet others of you were wondering about that point" will go a long way toward relieving anxiety and convincing others that they should not be afraid to speak. Alas how many teachers respond instead with,

"Didn't we cover that last time in great detail?"

"Is he the only one who couldn't do this problem?"

Critical answers like these discourage questioners. Putting out the welcome mat instead invites interaction.

STUDENT TIME-DELAY

Students always seem to be behind. If there's a weekly problem set, many will not start studying for it until the night before it is due; before that they will understand very little of what's been said in lecture during the week. No wonder they are silent.

You can deal with the problem three ways: ignore it, accept it, or fight it.

If you ignore it by pretending they are up-to-date, you'll find yourself doing most of the problem-choosing and talking, with class participation limited to just the few students who are prepared.

If you accept the situation, you'll probably feel it your duty to teach them what they haven't yet studied. It's a bad habit to get into, but if you do this, at least avoid straight lecturing—try to teach interactively, with questions and work they can do either together as a class, or individually or in small groups, with you going around and helping.

It's best of all to get your students to prepare for the recitation: best for the class as a whole and best for them as individuals. Some instructors give a very simple short weekly quiz which anyone can do after having looked at the week's reading. Students can grade each other's papers, and gain additional insight that way, since you will be discussing common mistakes.

Other teachers announce at the previous recitation a few problems that will be gone over at the next meeting. Some require a single problem to be handed in at each section meeting for grading. Often just a clear statement to your students of what you expect from them and what your plans are for the next section meeting can work wonders in encouraging them to prepare for class.

EYE CONTACT

Do you look at your students? Think how had it is to talk socially with someone who doesn't look at you. Nothing gives the "glass wall feeling" faster than to see a teacher explaining to the blackboard, the walls, the window, or a point about one foot over the students' heads.

If this describes you, one way to get started is to pick one or two students you know and address your remarks primarily to them. Once you get used to looking at them, you'll be able to branch out and look at the others. Eye contact will improve automatically as you get to know your students better—even very shy people are usually able to look at their friends when they talk with them.

LISTENING

To communicate, you have to be a good listener, because students often don't say exactly what they mean to say. If you give an elaborate response to an unasked question, it frustrates everyone. Try responding to a question with a question of your own, until you feel sure you know what it is that's being asked. If in doubt, enlist the aid of other students in the interpretation.

Q. I couldn't get problem 22 on page 253, could you work it?
A. Did you have trouble getting started, or was it something in the working out that bothered you?

Q. Is the gyroscope important?
A. Do you mean for your understanding of physics, or for the world of technology? Or do you mean for the exam next Wednesday?

THE STEAMROLLER

It's common to see recitation teachers carefully prepare a lot of problems and a lecture review for the hour, then realize in class it's a bit too much. So they shift into high gear and deliver it all as a fast lecture.

> Sir, could you explain that last step?
> If you're going to interrupt me with questions
> we'll never be able to cover the material.
> —math lecture

Such tactics "cover" the material, but they stifle interaction, and the class will give up and settle back in silence. Instead, relax and don't worry if you don't cover everything you've prepared; it's better to have a less tense atmosphere.

YOUR VOICE

Let's continue talking about the overall atmosphere in your class, since it controls the interaction so strongly. The way you say things gives powerful indications to students. Put a cassette recorder on the desk while you are teaching. Most people are shocked by the playback and don't believe what they hear. Here are some common speaking problems:

- Voice dropping into inaudibility at the end of each sentence

- A monotone or sing-song voice that makes concentration difficult

- Sentences interlarded with "O.K.?", "All right?" with no response expected

Your voice will give an unhappy emotional tone to your class if it sighs frequently with apparent boredom, or seems to express underlying anger or irritation. Again, listen to a playback to hear if this is you.

> Does Prof. R _____ realize that it's very hard to take notes after he puts us to sleep?

Certain habitual ways of speaking will seem like put-downs to your students and inhibit response. Phrases such as "it's obvious that" or "I think everyone should be able to see that" are very unsettling to insecure students. Think how much courage it takes to respond, "Well, I may be dumb, but I don't see how you did that . . ."

In the same category one can put sarcasm, which is unpleasant because it also plays with the student's feeling of self-worth. A teacher having excellent rapport with the class can get away with such phrases as "You're all geniuses so I know I won't have to explain this to you . . ." but it's too risky for the average class situation—it just isn't a joke to students who feel insecure.

FEEDBACK TIME

If despite your best efforts interaction is still sluggish, try taking 10 minutes off at the end of a period, putting your feet up, and asking the students in a general way what they think of the recitation. A good discussion can help a lot in clearing the air and pointing to the difficulties. Maybe there's something you didn't know. If they seem reluctant to talk, ask them to write down their thoughts and the next time you meet report back to them what the sentiments were.

KNOWING YOUR STUDENTS

Sometimes you'll be lucky—your recitation will have a few students who seem to spark everybody. But more typically, your class will just sit there in the beginning and won't seem too keen on talking. Don't worry about it. Communication is easier with people we know better, and as the students get to know each others' quirks and yours too, and as you start recognizing them in the halls, you'll find yourself relaxing and interaction will improve.

The section of this booklet titled The First Day has some suggestions on how to get to know your students and make them comfortable with each other. The important thing is to be patient and keep trying—they will respect your efforts and sooner or later will start responding.

Summary

Some of the points contained in this section are:

- Decide on the type of discussion that would be best for the class and tell them what that type is. (p. 32)

- Wait *at least* 3 seconds for a response after you've asked a question. (pp. 32, 35, 36)

- Assign specific tasks ahead of time. (pp. 32, 34)

- Give simple ground rules for the discussion. (p. 35)

- Get discussion started with a prepared first question. (p. 35)

- Guide group thinking; keep discussion on track. (p. 35)

- Periodically summarize what has been said. (p. 35)

- Allow time for a final summary at the end of the discussion. (p. 35)

- Divide the class into small groups (3 or 4) and ask them to consider a question. (p. 36)

- Ask easy review questions at first, to warm them up. (p. 38)

- Be a good listener. (p. 40)

- Ask for feedback. (p. 41)

4
Questioning

Early in September, Maureen goes to visit her advisor, Prof. Waldron.

"Excuse me, Pat? Can I bug you for a couple of minutes?"

"Sure, come on in. What can I do for you?"

"It's about my class. I've been teaching for a couple of years now, and I think I'm pretty good. My evaluations are always good, and my students seem to learn what I try to get across, so I feel I'm doing OK."

"That's what I've always thought. The couple of times that I've observed you, I've been quite impressed. So what's the trouble?"

"Well, I've met a couple of people who are TAs in other departments, and in talking to them about teaching, I've started to take a closer look at myself and what I think I need to work on. The area where I've always felt I've been the weakest is asking questions. It's easier for me now, but it was terrifically difficult for me when I started, and it's still pretty hard for me to do in class. What can you do for me?"

"Hmmm. Interesting. I've noticed in watching you teach that you could use a little work on questioning, but I never thought it bothered you. The best advice I can give is not to force it: follow the flow of the class. Let them do the work. Vary the kinds of questions you use; don't make them all like 'What did you think of this poem?' or 'Does anybody disagree with that?' Mix it up a bit. And don't be afraid of silence. If you ask a question, and don't get five hands waving in the air immediately, wait fifteen seconds or so. It seems like an eternity, but you'd be surprised what happens after a while. It seems like even longer to them.

"The best part of asking a lot of questions in class is that it forces the students to think a bit and, when it really works, they wind up teaching themselves. That's a great feeling."

"Wow," says Maureen. "I hadn't thought about it like that. Well, I'll work on it."

"In fact," says Pat, rummaging through a file drawer, "I've got a couple of those teaching-training guides around here, and they've got some stuff on questions. They're very helpful in thinking about kinds of questions besides the painfully obvious. Ahh, here they are. Maybe these will help."

"I'm sure they will. Thanks a lot."

"These TA friends of yours—what are they like?"

"Well, I've only known them a couple of weeks. Mercedes is from Venezuela, very nice, and in computer science. And then there's Steve. He's in history: a new grad student, a new TA, about 22, and thinks he's God's gift to higher education. He's a bit of jerk, but underneath it all, a nice guy. I think. They're a lot of fun."

"I'm glad you met them; they sound like they're helping you."

"Yeah, sometimes I don't need that kind of help, but, I like them. Thanks again, Pat. Take care."

QUESTIONS TO STUDENTS

An important lecture-breaking technique is questioning by the instructor to elicit student response. This approach can be used to identify student perceptions, to evaluate progress of the class, or to increase student involvement in learning. It varies the instructor's presentation and gives students a moment to work with the material presented, instead of just absorbing and organizing it. Following are some suggestions for in-class questioning.

- Give the students time to respond. If you ask a question that requires some reflection, allow the students time to think. One lecturer asks a demanding question, looks away from the class, counts silently to sixty, and then turns back to accept an answer.

- Avoid rapid reward for responding. Rapid reward means calling on the first person who raises a hand or approving immediately a correct answer. Both prevent other students from constructing their answers or from evaluating the correctness of the given answer.

- Call on different people. If one student always has a hand in the air before you even finish the question, look at that student and say that you also want to give other people a chance to answer. After several questions answered by the same group of faster students, announce that you want to take an answer from someone who has not had a chance to answer anything today.

- Be supportive to the person who gives a wrong answer. A student who gives a wrong answer must be made to feel confident about answering other questions. *Never ridicule a student.* Try to avoid saying flatly "that is wrong," although you cannot let the rest of the class assume the wrong answer is correct. Some helpful reactions are "Will you go into that a bit more? Can you explain how you arrived at your conclusion?" (The student may reveal the source of the error, which you can quickly correct and explain that the conclusion did naturally follow from that flaw.) "You're right about one part (state it), but let me explain again how we can apply that principle." "I know that (the point) can be a difficult concept to grasp. How many other people made the same mistake?" "That is a good starting point. Who else can add to it?"

- Vary the cognitive level of questions. This gives students practice in thinking at different levels and for different purposes.

- Ask questions that encourage students to form hypotheses or explore "if-then" relationships. With this kind of tactic, one student can extend the work of another, and so involve much of the class in the discussion.

- Avoid programmed answers. Programmed answers come from questions that contain the answer. For example, "Was a cause of the French revolution the great dichotomy between the rich and the poor?" Such questions, which often evoke only a "yes" or "no" answer, may even lead to sheer guessing. More insightful questions begin with "what", "why", or "how".

Humphreys, L. and Wickersham, B. (1986) *A handbook of resources for new instructors at UTK.* Learning Research Center, University of Tennessee, Knoxville.

- Use the following kinds of questions: inductive questions to lead students to synthesize and generalize, probing questions to cause students to deepen their ideas or verbalize justifications and conclusions, and comparison and contrast questions to help students develop recognition of similarities and differences.

Restrict questions, for example, in a large lecture where too many questions would inhibit class progress. In such cases, however, encourage students to share their questions and comments with you outside of class. There are several good techniques to encourage student participation. Just as asking the right kinds of questions can elicit the kinds of student responses you want, the way you answer questions and accept comments can influence the kind and number of questions and remarks students offer. Following are suggestions for stimulating class discussion.

- Restate complex or inaudible questions for the whole class, or ask the student to do so.

- Listen carefully and show it. Look attentive, select key points and summarize, and test your understanding by asking a follow-up question or by rephrasing.

- Do not be afraid to admit you don't know an answer. Students will accept that if you are willing to seek the answer and explain it later, or if you tell them you are going to try to solve the problem in front of them. You can also seek the aid of other students in the class.

- If you see potential in a comment, draw out the student by asking him or her to elaborate or to apply the point in new ways.

- Build on the student's point. After taking one comment, list it on the board and solicit other remarks. Withhold judgment until you have several contributions listed, then ask the class to regroup them. In this way, the work becomes a product of the whole class, and students still perceive less significant points as being contributions to the whole.

- Have students nominate topics for discussion at the beginning of class. If the section material lends itself to open-ended questions, have a brainstorming session.

- If a discussion group is large, divide it into smaller units, working independently. Move from group to group, offering guidance and asking and answering questions where appropriate.

In summary, there is no "right" technique for dealing with individual student questions, responses, and remarks. If you make a student feel good about contributing, you show others in class that they, too, can find participation rewarding.

USING QUESTIONS IN TEACHING

Questioning as an instructional technique has been recommended to teachers since Socrates first used it to draw out ideas from students. A steady stream of books and monographs on the "art of questioning" has appeared over the years. These attest to the belief that appropriate questioning behavior is an important teacher characteristic. A common theme throughout the literature is that questioning is a means by which she elicits higher order mental processes such as critical judgment. It was John Dewey who pointed out that thinking itself was questioning. It would seem that the critical requirement for a "good" classroom question is that the question prompt the student to use ideas rather than just remember them. The generally accepted premise is that the form of the question serves as the stimulus for eliciting certain kinds of cognitive activities which may range from simple recall to highly complex inferences from data.

Thus one of the first things a potential questioner must learn to recognize is the fact that questions have different characteristics. Among the many types of questions we may distinguish two, those which are factual or lower order and those which are more complex or higher order questions. Some people break down the higher order category into sub-categories such as interpretation, analysis, synthesis, evaluation, etc. The reason for attempting to identify different kinds of questions is quite simple: it is believed that different types of questions produce different kinds of cognitive responses on the part of the students.

Not all the responses of students are cognitive. Some responses can be seen through simple observation of classrooms. For example, when a teacher asks a simple memory question like, "Who was the sixteenth President?" you often notice students wildly raising their hand and/or you can hear such sounds as "ooh-ooh" and others which in general try to attract the teacher's attention, in order to be called upon. The students are *sure* they know the answer. They are sure they can deliver a response for which the teacher will respond positively to them. On the other hand, when a question is highly complex, students will often ask for clarification of the question or show signs of puzzlement or tentativeness in the hand-raising that occurs. These are observable behavioral indicators of the simplicity or complexity of the various questions that are being asked. Thus even through simple observation, and without any access to the cognitive structure of students, we can often see the effects of questions.

Questions can also be asked in certain kinds of sequences. For example a number of factual questions in a row can be used to establish a certain data base. This can be followed by a higher-order question which incorporates material from the established factual data base. Other strategies might call for simple alternation of lower-order and higher-order questions. The "correctness" or "incorrectness" of using the various strategies is unknown. What is desirable is that the teacher recognize that such strategies do exist.

Source unknown

46

HIGHER ORDER QUESTIONS

Higher order questions are questions that cannot be answered merely from memory or by simple sensory description. This kind of question requires abstract thinking on the part of the student. It requires him to go beyond the factual or descriptive statement and learn to generalize, to relate facts in meaningful patterns, to compare and contrast concepts or principles, to make inferences, to perceive causes and effects. Higher order questions call for the discovery of concepts rather than for their definition. They prompt the student to use ideas rather than just remember them.

The key word related to higher order questions is *why*. The question "Why?" requires the student to go beyond the factual or descriptive answer. However, such questions do not necessarily demand more than memory. The question "Why did the Civil War break out?" is merely a factual or descriptive question if the student is expected simply to repeat what he was told in a lecture or textbook. That same question would be a higher order question if the student were expected to identify the major causes himself, after considering a variety of conditions and events preceding the war. The salient feature of higher order questions is that they lead students to figure out answers rather than remember them.

Each student brings a different frame of reference into the classroom, based on the sum of his knowledge, experience, and values. Consequently, a higher order question for one student might be a factual question for another. For example, asking one student to prove that two triangles are congruent might be asking him to perform a mathematical operation that is new to him. Asking the same question of another student might be asking him simply to repeat an operation he knows by heart.

Here are six specific functions that higher order questions may perform:

1. Asking for Evaluations

Questions asking for evaluations resemble divergent questions in that there is no "right" answer. They deal with "matters of judgment, value and choice." Norris Sanders states that any idea can be evaluated in two main steps. The first step is to set up appropriate standards. The second is to judge how closely the idea or object being evaluated meets these standards. If no standards are offered, or if they are only suggested, then a question is considered evaluative. It is evaluative because the respondent must himself set standards against which to evaluate whatever is in question. An evaluative answer is always somewhat subjective. Either the standard cannot be proved to be correct, or the idea or object cannot be judged with reference to the standard's criteria. The following examples of evaluative questions imply that the student must set up standards to use in answering the question:

a. Which of the two cartoons do you believe contributes the most to an understanding of the problems of the American Indian in the twentieth century?
b. Assuming equal resources, who would you rate as the more skillful general, Robert E. Lee, or Ulysses S. Grant? Why?

Source unknown

47

2. Asking for Inferences

Inferences always involve either deduction or induction. *Deduction* is reasoning from a general principle to a particular case covered by the principle. Deduction is essentially a logical operation: if it is true that all men are mortal, then if Socrates is a man it follows necessarily that Socrates is mortal. *Induction* is the discovery of a general principle from a collection of specific facts: if the sun has been observed to rise every day since the beginning of recorded history, one may induce the generalization that the sun rises every day. This operation of induction is not essentially logical. As Hume (from whom this example of the sun is taken) long ago showed, there is no logical necessity that the sun will indeed rise tomorrow. However, logic does figure in induction, though not essentially. When a generalization occurs to someone, he usually judges its worth by returning, through deduction, to specific cases covered by the generalization. He reasons to himself, "If this generalization is true, then it should follow that such-and-such is the case." If "such-and-such" proves not to be the case, he rejects the generalization. He can never prove the generalization to be true, but he can corroborate it. The more instances in which the generalization is not shown to be false, the more confidence he can have in it. In science, this process of testing generalizations (called hypotheses) is done formally in most cases. In everyday life, the process, when it occurs, is usually automatic or quite casual.

Question *a* asks for a deductive inference, and question *b* asks for an inductive inference.

   a.   Why does wet laundry, hung on a clothesline, dry faster on a hot summer day than on a cool autumn day?
   b.   We have examined the qualities these many world leaders have in common. What might we conclude, in general, about the qualities necessary for leadership? Why?

3. Asking for Comparisons

A comparison question asks a student to determine if ideas or objects are similar, dissimilar, unrelated, or contradictory. We can make several different kinds of comparisons. The simplest asks whether or not two or more ideas or objects are identical, as in example *a*. Another kind, example *b*, tests the degree of similarity between ideas or objects. A third kind asks the student to relate sets of ideas on similar points. Example *c* is such a question. But, as Norris Sanders has argued, the most challenging comparison is one where the student is free to choose which aspects of things he will compare. Example *d* is this fourth kind of question.

   a.   Is a mussel the same thing as a clam?
   b.   What are the similarities and differences between London and New York City?
   c.   Compare the life of the bumble bee with that of an ant.
   d.   What is the connection between a representative form of government and the American Revolution?

4. Asking for Application of Concepts or Principles

A concept is defined as a classification of events or objects that have common characteristics. A principle is defined as the relationship between two or more concepts. Teachers can test understanding of a concept or principle by asking the student to use it in a context different from that in which he learned it. If the student uses the concept correctly, the teacher is reasonably assured that the student understands.

   a.   How is Newton's Third Law demonstrated in the movement of a balloon when air is let out of it?
   b.   Can you think of another example which fits this definition?

5. Asking for Problem-Solving

Problem-solving questions require a student to use previously-learned knowledge to solve a problem new to him. Questions of this nature require the student to see relationships between his knowledge and the problem. Often these questions demand a great deal of creativity from the student. One of the difficult steps in solving a problem is to decide which facts or skills are relevant. When students do not know where to begin or what knowledge will be relevant, they can be given hints or directions by the teacher.

    a. Given this information, how would you go about solving the food shortage problem?

    b. Can you prove that these two paintings were created by the same artist?

6. Asking for Cause and Effect

These questions require the student to perceive causal relationships between events and persons, objects, ideas, or other events. They ask the student to find a link that connects one with another.

    a. If I were to heat this water, what would be the result?

    b. If the wheat crop all over the world failed, what foods would be missing from our diet?

Higher order questions stimulate students to go beyond the factual level of thinking in order to generalize, infer, evaluate, and perceive relationships. Imaginative use of higher order questions can enliven an otherwise dull classroom discussion. A teacher should know what kind of thinking he wishes to stimulate and should select the appropriate kind of question. Sustained higher order questioning is difficult. But practice combined with diligent study will result in a more versatile and effective questioner.

PROBING QUESTIONS

Teacher:	Would you say that nationalism in Africa is now greater or less than it was twenty years ago?
Student:	Greater.
Teacher:	Right. Why is that so?
Student:	Because there are more nations now.
Teacher:	That's right, too, but's only part of it. Can anyone else give me some more reasons?
Class:	(Silence)
Teacher:	Well, basically, it's because . . .

A teacher wants his class to discuss a topic. He asks a question and receives a cursory answer that adds next to nothing to the discussion. The discussion drags. It evolves into an unprepared lecture. In many cases, this is the teacher's fault. He may ask questions that are embarrassingly simple. However, it may be that his students are shy, afraid of answering incorrectly, or just naturally taciturn.

Effective teachers keep discussions going by asking questions that require more than superficial answers. They do this in two ways. One is to forestall superficial answers by asking questions to which such answers cannot be given. This is what higher order questions do. The other approach is based on techniques that may be used after a student has given a superficial response. By probing, the teacher requires the student to go beyond his first response. His cue is the student's response. Once it has occurred, the teacher, instead of advancing to another question, probes the student's response by means of one of the techniques outlined below.

More than any other skill in this cluster, probing will require you to give an unrehearsed response. Because the probe depends on the student's response, you will rarely be able to prepare probing questions in advance of the lesson. However, by practicing probing questions with a variety of responses, you can develop a repertoire of question formats to apply when appropriate in the classroom.

The probing techniques outlined below can be used in any situation where student participation is necessary to realize the goals of the lesson. A given technique, of course, may be appropriate in one situation but not in another.

1. The teacher seeks clarification. He may ask the student for more information, or clarification, by saying:

    a. "What, exactly, do you mean?"
    b. "Please rephrase that statement."
    c. "Could you elaborate on that point?"
    d. "What do you mean by the term . . . ?"

Source unknown

2. The teacher seeks to increase the student's critical awareness. He wants the student to justify his response. Examples of appropriate probing questions are:

   a. "What are you assuming?"
   b. "What are your reasons for thinking that is so?"
   c. "Is that all there is to it?"
   d. "How many questions are we trying to answer here?"
   e. "How would an opponent of this point of view respond?"

3. The teacher refocuses the response. If a student has given a satisfactory response, it might seem unnecessary to probe it. However, the teacher could use this opportunity to refocus on a related issue. Examples of probing questions that might also refocus the responses are:

   a. "If this is true, what are the implications for . . . ?"
   b. "How does John's answer relate to . . . ?"
   c. "Can you relate this to . . . ?"
   d. "Let's analyze that answer."

4. The teacher prompts the student. The teacher gives the student hints to help him answer the question:

Teacher:	"John, what's the square root of 94?"
John:	"I don't know."
Teacher:	"Well, what's the square root of 100?"
John:	"Ten."
Teacher:	"And the square root of 81?"
John:	"Nine."
Teacher:	"Then what do we know about the square root of 94?"
John:	"It's between nine and ten."

5. The teacher redirects the question. This is not a probing technique, per se, but it does help bring other students into the discussion quickly, while still using probing techniques. The teacher changes the interaction from himself and one student to himself and another student:

Teacher:	"What is the theme of Hemingway's *Old Man and the Sea*?"
Sam:	"It's about an old man's courage in catching a fish."
Teacher:	"Mary, do you agree?"
or:	"Mary, do you think it's that simple?"
or:	"Mary, can you elaborate on Sam's answer?"

These techniques have two main characteristics in common in that they are initiated by the teacher immediately after the student has responded, and they require the student to think beyond his initial response.

REINFORCEMENT

A teacher plays a key role in the creation of desirable learning conditions in the classroom. As Sears and Hilgard have said:

> First, teacher personality and behavior act through a kind of contagion, in which the teacher becomes a model for appropriate behavior. The principles at work here are those of imitation and identification. Second, the teacher, as an administrator of rewards and punishments, wields power and creates a structure in which learning occurs. Here the principles are the more usual ones of positive and negative reinforcement.[1]

The teacher's role as a positive reinforcer is the focus of this exercise. Positive reinforcement of a behavior increases the likelihood that the behavior will recur. If a student behaves in a desirable way, immediate positive reinforcement increases the probability of his continuing to do so.

The difficulty is that the strength and quality of any reinforcer varies with the student to whom it is applied. No teacher can know exactly what will positively reinforce each of the thirty or so students in each of his five or six classes. It is impossible for him to acquire this information from the science of human behavior at its present stage of development. Tests may eventually be developed to furnish such information, but that day is a long way off. Hence, the contemporary teacher must rely primarily on the words, phrases, and gestures that experience has shown to work as reinforcers in most cases. In addition, he should notice his students' individual traits. These will suggest that certain reinforcers might be more effective than others.

Besides directly increasing learning reinforcement is an effective means of increasing student participation in classroom activities. Participation, in turn, usually increases learning. When students take part in classroom activities, they are more likely to become involved with the material than when they do not take part. They pay closer attention. An experiment conducted at Stanford University has shown that teachers who often reinforce their students for joining in class discussions draw more participation from their students than teachers who reinforce infrequently. If teachers use a few reinforcement techniques, they should significantly increase their students' participation.

Four kinds of positive reinforcement are available to the teacher:

1. Positive verbal reinforcement occurs when the teacher immediately follows a desired student response with such comments as "Good," "Fine," "Excellent," "Correct," or other statements indicating satisfaction with the response.

Source unknown

[1]Pauline S. Sears and Ernest R. Hilgard. "The Teacher's Role in the Motivation of the Learner," *Theories of Learning and Instruction.* The Sixty-Third Yearbook of the National Society for the Study of Education, Part I (Chicago, 1964), p. 206.

2. Positive nonverbal reinforcement occurs when the teacher, in responding to a desired student response, nods his head affirmatively, smiles, moves toward the student, or keeps his eyes on the student while paying close attention to the student's words. The teacher may write the student's response on the chalkboard or otherwise nonverbally indicate pleasure at the student's response.

3. Positively qualified reinforcement occurs when the teacher differentially reinforces, either verbally or nonverbally, the acceptable parts of a response, as in the following example:

Teacher:	John, how is yellow fever transmitted?
John:	I think it is transmitted by flies.
Teacher:	You're right; it's an insect that carries the disease, but it isn't a fly. What is it?

4. Delayed reinforcement occurs when the teacher emphasizes positive aspects of students' responses by redirecting class attention to earlier contributions by a student, as in this example:

Teacher:	Class, which side would you have expected the English industrialists to support during the Civil War: the South or the North?
Class:	The South. The North. (class is divided)
Teacher:	Jane, do you remember earlier in the class you mentioned one of the leading industries in England?
Class:	Yes. It was clothes-making.
Teacher:	Does that give anyone a hint?
Class:	They supported the South because they wanted the cotton the South grew for making clothes.
Teacher:	Good, Sam. That was a good deduction.

Note here that both Jane and Sam have been reinforced by the teacher: Jane, because the teacher drew the students' attention to her earlier contribution and asked her to repeat her statement; Sam, because the teacher praised him for deducing the answer to the original question.

Shy students who rarely join in class discussion present a difficult problem, but not an insoluble one. Gradually, these students can be encouraged to become involved. When a teacher notices a shy student looking at him or attending what is going on in class, the teacher should reinforce this behavior by nodding or smiling at the student; in effect, the teacher says he is pleased that the student is paying attention. The teacher can further encourage this student's participation by asking him easy questions. This insures that the student will have successful experiences when he first begins to participate. If the teacher extends this process over a period of time, the student should take part more. Each time he participates, he should be reinforced, until he reaches a normal level of involvement.

Most of us, in our normal conversations, use a very narrow range of reinforcers. "Good," "Uh-huh," "Right," and "Yeah," are frequently used as reinforcers. It is hoped that this exercise will enable you to extend your range of both verbal and nonverbal reinforcers. The possible range is a very broad one. It extends from such exclamations as "Fantastic!" and "Tremendous!" through statements such as "Excellent," "Very good," "Good," and "Yes," to mild gestures such as a slight nod of the head. Each of these reinforcers should convey a different feeling and meaning. Your task is to enlarge your repertoire of reinforcers and to apply them sensitively. Saying "Tremendous!" to an average response, or even to a very good response, is ridiculous. Reinforcement must correspond to the adequacy of the student's response. A few of the reinforcing statements and actions required by the practice exercises may feel uncomfortable to you at first. They may seem foreign to your interaction style. However, as you develop your range of reinforcers, you should, in the long run, have a greater effect on your students.

USING QUESTIONS TO ENHANCE CLASSROOM LEARNING

Introduction

Many teachers unwittingly and subtly stymy students' intellectual development and growth of self-confidence by the ways they use and phrase questions. Rather than posing questions which provoke thoughts, evoke expression, encourage discussions, initiate arguments, raise further questions, and enable students to ask without embarrassment about what they do not understand, these teachers use and phrase vague, dead-end, or threatening questions, or suggest their own answers to the questions they pose. Conversely, instructors who have learned the skills of effective questioning are able to teach by their own example how to acquire and classify information, and to think logically. They change students from passive classroom spectators to active, creative participants in the learning process. Through the use of examples, this paper will attempt to help the reader become aware of how questions can subvert or enhance teaching goals.

In Part One, examples of actual classroom questions will be classified and analyzed; in Part Two, the components of an effective type of questioning strategy will be discussed; Part Three will offer some methods for using questions to stimulate thinking and enhance classroom learning.

It is my strong belief that learning is enhanced when the learner does something with the material presented. In this spirit, I have designed tasks throughout this paper to engage each reader and reinforce the ideas under investigation.

PART ONE:
Classification and Analysis of Some Actual Classroom Questions

In a classroom whose climate is characterized by openness, a respect for ideas, and flexibility of teaching methods, students may well respond freely to half-phrased, poorly articulated, fuzzily worded questions. Too, in a class of highly motivated, interested students, ofttimes an instructor need do little else than suggest a topic, or pose a problem. Yet these atypical situations should not blind us to the need for good plans and thoughtful questions in structuring positive learning experiences for all students all the time.Few instructors would quarrel with the statement that questions should provoke thought and evoke expression. (Stevens, 1912). Yet my own analyses of questions taken verbatim from classroom dialogues indicate that many faculty question their students in ways which confuse thinking and suppress responses. Five such types of questions are described here: the "Dead-End" or Yes-No Question; the "Chameleon" Question; the Question with a Programmed Answer; the Put-Down Question; and the Fuzzy Question. Those observing videotaped recordings have picked up the more obvious consequences of each of these question-types: students' facial expressions show puzzlement, annoyance, despair; their hands gesture in confusion; they shrug their shoulders and raise their eyebrows; and they often greet these questions with an almost total lack of verbal response. In

Napell, S. (1978). Using questions to enhance classroom learning. *Education* 99 (2).

each instance a change of wording and/or pace can result in a radically altered response. These will be suggested as each type is discussed.

THE "DEAD-END" (OR YES-NO) QUESTION

Examples:

a. Does everyone remember Snell's Law?
b. Dr. Trilling told you why they use this angle to design Polaroid sun glasses, right?
c. Does everyone understand what shifts the demand curves and the supply curves around?
d. Do you all see the difference between long-run and short-run costs?
e. Does scale mean anything at all?
f. Now do you see why I substituted the value of 0 in this equation?
g. Do you see how in *this* instance it would be different?

When asked about the intent of these questions, instructors usually respond that they want to make sure that their students do understand these subjects. However, few wait long enough for students to reply; most accept as evidence of general understanding one or two murmured yesses. And, even *were* everyone to respond with a "yes," what would the instructor *really* have found out? If we look over the representative seven "Dead-End" Questions, we can see that a slight change of wording, plus a willingness to wait for an answer would elicit responses telling the instructor more precisely what he[1] wants to know.

For example:

a. Does everyone remember Snell's Law?
a'. What does Snell's Law tell us?

b. Dr. Trilling told you why they use this angle to design Polaroid sun glasses, right?
b'. What did Dr. Trilling suggest was the reason for using this angle to design Polaroid sun glasses?

c. Does everyone understand what shifts the demand curves and the supply curves around?
c'. Let's list (or review) together some of the factors which cause the demand curves and the supply curves to shift.

For your own practice, turn back to the remaining four examples of the "Dead-End" type of question, and ask yourself what it is that the students need to explain. Then, try rephrasing the question to give you this feedback and give them the opportunity to express their understanding of, or problems with, the material.

THE "CHAMELEON" (OR RUN-ON) QUESTION

Examples:

a. What does it mean that he's a Scholastic?. . . Do you remember what Starr said about Scholasticism?. . . What did Chrystal say?. . . Well, who is this Scholastic studying?

---

[1]The reader is asked to accept the conventional use of the pronoun "his" and "him" as a reference to both sexes in order that the distraction of the him/her constructions may be avoided.

b. What abut Thomas Hutchinson?. . . Where is he writing this?. . . How is he writing?. . . Would he be likely to join the mob?. . . How much of an unruly mob is it?

c. Now we have this table, what are we doing?. . . What's the elimination that we need?. . . Last time, didn't we have the returned earnings of the parent and company sales?. . . What's the difference *this* time?

d. What is a demand curve?. . . Where does it come from?. . . Remember, we discussed one thing first: utility. . . What's marginal utility?

e. What kinds of things did they attempt to do?. . . Where did they attack?. . . You mentioned living conditions, what about that?

f. Now, what kind of Physics was going on at that time?. . . Did anyone have any hypothesis then?

g. How does one design a park?. . . Do you walk it?. . . Should it be on the periphery?. . . Should it be within the central city?. . . What examples have we of each?

h. Who sees a community?. . . What's under that tree?. . . Do you see a boundary between grass and litter country?

An examination of this second type of question illumines several of its characteristics. Each "question" although asked virtually in one breath, is in reality a series of questions; the first question of the series is different from the last. The questioner seems unclear about what it is that he is asking since each succeeding question requires a somewhat different answer.

The responses to Chameleon Questions are varied. Most students are often so unsure of what is being asked that they will sit silently to see what will happen; some quickly answer the easiest, the first, or the last question of the group. Some brave soul or those "on the spot" may ask, "What was your question?" or, "Would you mind repeating the question?"

Videotaped replay reveals a typical consequence of this questioning pattern. Hands will go up in response to the first question, a few will go down during the second, and those hands remaining up gradually will get lower and lower as the instructor finally concludes with a question very different from the one for which the hands were initially raised.

There are, in addition, subtle unobservable consequences of Chameleon Questions. Students barraged with many questions, all asked at once, are denied time to reflect and formulate answers. Their thinking does not follow any logical progression but, at best, jumps with the instructor's from topic to topic. They are not encouraged to express their thoughts, but rather discouraged from doing so as the thrust of the question changes so rapidly.

Assimilation of ideas and their orderly expression demand time. Instructors can model logical thinking and orderly expression by making sure that lesson goals are apparent in their questions, preparing questions ahead of time, then pausing to offer students sufficient wait-time[1]. These behaviors encourage students to suggest their own ideas, confront each other's opinions, raise further questions, and become active participants in classroom communication. (Napell, 1975).

To practice avoiding Chameleon Questions, look back at the eight examples listed and figure out how you would ask one clearly stated question. For example:

a. What does it mean that he's a Scholastic?. . . Do you remember what Starr said about Scholasticism?. . . What did Chrystal say?. . . Well, who is this Scholastic studying?

---

[1]"Wait-time" is defined as the amount of time after an initial question has been posed before the teacher answers it himself; repeats, rephrases, or adds further information to the question; or accepts an answer from a student. (Moriber, 1951).

a'. Both Professors Starr and Chrystal offered slightly different definitions of Scholasticism. Look over your notes at their definitions, and try to come up with one that will include their main points plus your own understanding of what this term means.

THE QUESTION WITH A PROGRAMMED ANSWER

Examples:

a. "What thoughts have you about impeachment? Do you think the proceedings are too lengthy? That partisan politics play too great a role? Is there enough evidence?"

b. "What role does collective bargaining play in higher education? Do we have any indications as to the effect of collective bargaining on curriculum? Is it going to rigidify it?"

c. "What reasons do you have to use that formula? Was it suggested in the homework chapter? Had you ever used it before? Or seen it used in this context?"

d. "What happens when we add the sums of the rows? Do we get skewed results?"

e. "Look at this shrub and tell me, what observations can you make? Do you see the dead stems? Are they damaged from insect feeding?"

This type of question programs the answer: it not only deprives the respondent from expressing his own thoughts by steering him towards the answers that the questioner expects, but also conveys the message that there is really little interest in what he thinks or says. Those who practice this pattern usually have altruistic justifications (e.g., "Silence after the posing of a question is embarrassing to the student;" "I feel impelled to help out by suggesting clues"), but they need to ask themselves honestly: "Is it I or the student who is uncomfortable after a second or two of silence?"; "Do I have confidence in the students' ability to think about the question and formulate a response?" and, most important, "Am I more interested in what the student has to say or in determining which of *my* answers he prefers?" Programming can be an effective tool in guiding students' thinking, suggesting possibilities, or modeling logical thought processes. However, it is important to be aware of its limiting effect when the goal is to court a wide variety of ideas. If yours is this latter goal, try asking one relatively open-ended question and waiting to hear the students' responses. For example, look back at the first question of this type. It can be changed to a question which allows the student to express his own ideas by asking: "What thoughts have you about impeachment?" and pausing to allow the student to express his own ideas. In this way you indicate your interest in his ideas and model more effective questioning and listening behavior. A willingness to listen helps to create in the classroom a community of learners in place of a super-ordinate-subordinate relationship between teacher and class.

THE PUT-DOWN QUESTION

Examples:

a. OK, Professor Brown went over this twice in lecture yesterday, and I just did it on the board. Any more questions?

b. Who can reword her answer the way you think I would say it?

c. Anybody so confident in his answer that he wants to come up and put it on the board?

d. That was one explanation, yes, but what's another more obvious one?

e. Does anybody know "King Lear" pretty well here?

f. Obviously, it's simply the same Lorentz we've used four times. Any questions?

g. I think the exam problems were pretty straightforward. Any questions?

h. Problem three, was there any question on that? We gave you the solutions, you just differentiated the first one; I don't think there should be any problems on that or the rest. Are there?

Students need to be able to ask questions, for "the questions we ask act like a lens clarifying or distorting information relevant and necessary to us." (Burkhart, 1969). The Put-Down Question is often used as a ruse: the instructor really does not want any further questions. The wording represents a dare to the most brazen, the most hardened, or the most desperate. Thus, instructors subtly dissuade students from asking for necessary clarification. How much more honest to invite those with further questions to meet during office hours . . . or to avoid asking for further questions entirely. Put-Down Questions are often indications of an instructor's ego-needs' taking precedence over his students' learning needs.

THE FUZZY QUESTION

Example:

a. Do you sort of understand what is the principle behind this?
b. Did you notice this business of friendship?
c. How do you suppose one would get such a thing as that?
d. How about plane mirrors?
e. Does everybody feel somewhat like that?
f. The question is, can we prove that? Who got some ideas on that?
g. Does that explain what's going on?
h. Anybody care to explain that in different words?
i. Let's do it for the globular cluster.
j. Is it in all red giants?

An important function of the classroom teaching-learning process is offering students opportunities to use the new vocabulary of the course. As instructors, we can model accurate usage of new terms not only by using them in our own discussion and responses, but also by using them in our questions. Students are better able and more willing to respond to our questions when we state clearly what it is we are asking and simultaneously offer some tools with which they can construct an answer. Compare the following pairs of questions for clarity and the assistance they offer:

a. Do you sort of understand the principle behind this?
a'. How would you describe the principle which accounts for these graph fluctuations?

b. Did you notice this business of friendship?
b'. In the Iliad, Homer often refers to the friendship between men. How would you explain his concept of friendship using the examples he cites?

c. How do you suppose one would get such a thing as that?
c'. Using what we've just learned about alleles, how could you account for the offspring's having these combinations?

DIVERGENT QUESTIONS

The kind of question probably asked least often in the classroom is what has been variously called the *divergent*, the *heuristic*, or the *creative* question. Such a question has no "right" answer. It is an open-ended question, requiring students to use both concrete and abstract thinking to determine for themselves an appropriate response. Students are free to explore the problem in whatever direction they prefer; they are asked to think creatively, to leave the comfortable confines of the known and reach out for the unknown. This is often more uncomfortable for the teacher than it is for the students, since the answers he or she receives cannot be classified as either right or wrong. But this is the fascination and challenge of divergent questioning. The teacher and the students free themselves to explore hypotheses and possibilities.

The following are divergent questions:

1. What might happen to our economy if the gasoline automobile were declared illegal for smog-prevention reasons?

2. If you were stuck on a desert island and the only tool you had was a screwdriver, what uses might you make of it?

3. What might happen if Congress passed a law preventing the manufacture and sale of cigarettes in the United States?

4. How would the story be different if the character had been strong and healthy instead of disabled?

5. How would life in the San Francisco Bay Area be different if the bay were filled in?

6. In what way would history have been changed had the Spanish Armada defeated the English in 1588?

Source unknown

Summary

Some of the points contained in this section are:

- Give students sufficient time to respond. (p. 44)

- Avoid "rapid reward." (p. 44)

- Call on different people. (p. 44)

- Be supportive to students who give incorrect answers. (p. 44)

- Vary the cognitive level of the questions. (p. 44)

- Restate complex or inaudible questions for the class. (p. 45)

- Don't be afraid to admit that you don't know an answer. (p. 45)

- Build on a student's point. (p. 45)

- Different kinds of questions call for different kinds of answers. (pp. 46, 47)

- Higher order questions may perform six specific functions. (pp. 47-49)

- Probing questions require the student to go beyond the first response. (pp. 50-51)

- There are at least four kinds of positive reinforcement. (pp. 52-54)

- Reinforce students for answering questions. (p. 52)

- Avoid "dead-end," "chameleon," "programmed," "put-down," and "fuzzy" questions. (pp. 56-59)

- Divergent questions require both concrete and abstract thinking. (p. 60)

5
Labs

"You know what I am going to enjoy the most about this year?" Mercedes asks one night early in the semester.

"Not living in the graduate dorm?" asks Steve. "I'm there now, and it's not quite what I expected."

"Besides that. I don't have to supervise the computer lab any more!"

"Was it really as bad as all that?"

"No, but it got to be a nuisance at times. Actually, most of the time I sort of liked it. The biggest thing, though, was that everyone expected me to know everything. Why the printer didn't work. Why the software was missing. Why the mainframe system had gone down. A lot of the time I'd know, but when I didn't, I felt bad."

"There's this guy Charles living down the hall from me who's a new Chem TA this year and he's doing labs, too. It sounds kind of different from what you did, though. He's got to prepare demonstration labs for his students and then supervise them as they try to do the experiments themselves. He doesn't mind it, but he said the preparation was the key—once he wasn't quite ready because he hadn't had enough time, and the whole thing was a disaster."

"It is different in a computer lab, but we all have to deal with students on a one-to-one basis and be able to answer questions on all kinds of levels. It can be very stimulating at times. I'm still glad I don't have to do it this year, though."

"Yeah, but who is running it now? Do they know what they're doing? Like how to do the assignment you gave out this morning?"

"Oh, no! I forgot to leave a copy with the monitor! I gotta go!" said Mercedes, as she tore off towards the lab, leaving Steve snickering over his beer.

LABS

Classroom control is fairly easy at the college level. Students are conditioned to "good behavior" in the lecture setting and usually in the discussion setting too. However, some real management problems seem to arise in laboratory or studio situations. I have learned about laboratory management that:

1. It is desirable to maintain a lesser degree of control than in a discussion; one cannot realistically expect a quiet, orderly lab session.

2. Here is one control pattern which works: start each lab period in a fairly formal manner. Gradually loosen up during the session (especially in those four-hour labs!) The object here is to end the session somewhat short of chaos.

3. Expect to be stricter earlier in the quarter than towards the end. You can't fight the second law of thermodynamics: disorder *will* tend to increase with time.

4. In physics, the laboratory grade is usually only 10 to 15% of the student's final grade: many students who realize this will socialize excessively at the expense of their work. With only 10% of the student's grade available for blackmail, the TA lacks sufficient leverage to make the students perform, and therefore, shouldn't use grades as a threat.

5. Most important, the majority of college students will respect an instructor who is familiar with the experiment. The following suggestions are offered.

    a. *Perform* the entire *experiment* in advance—there is no guarantee it's going to work as advertised in the lab manual.

    b. Read and study the *theory* on which the experiment is based—otherwise, some student will hit you with a question you can't handle.

    c. Wherever possible point out interesting historical aspects of the experiment, e.g. "Galileo did this whole thing using a cathedral lantern for a pendulum and his pulse for a watch!" Historical notes keep students from bitching too much about the lack of quality in their experimental apparati. This silences the student who figures the experiment is a waste of his/her time: "If it's good enough for Isaac Newton, or Count Rutherford, or Volta, Ampere, or any of those other guys with something named after them, then it must be good enough for me."

    d. Finally, do some research into the relevance of the experiment, either the technique being taught, or applications of the theory being demonstrated.

The most important thing the TA can do to insure that the lab session runs smoothly is to come very well prepared. The TA must know exactly *what* the students are supposed to learn and *why* they have to learn these things. This includes being thoroughly familiar with the details of the experiment and knowing *why* the procedure is done in a particular way, as well as *what* the student should get out of it. It is your responsibility to be familiar with the

---

Morrow, R. (1976). *What every TA should know.* In *The TA at UCLA: A handbook for teaching assistants. (1977-78).* The Regents of the University of California.

principles behind each experiment, which usually means knowing how the experiments tie in with the lecture material. *Tell* your students what you expect them to be learning. It's not a secret.

Laboratory rules should be strictly enforced because they are entirely for the safety of the class. Your own adherence to the rules about eating, smoking, etc. and firm discipline when safety is at issue should be sufficient to avoid serious problems.

If you are cooperative and show your students respect, they will generally return the same. It usually helps to encourage them to be alert and relaxed and to help each other as much as they can. Frequent short quizzes (graded or not) tend to improve their preparation and keep them more alert.

Although many TAs tend to stay in the front of the classroom, there are substantial advantages to circulating through your lab. You can demonstrate proper techniques and help with problems and questions before they blossom into failure or catastrophe. Best of all, you can get to know your class on a more personal basis.

Finally, relax and enjoy yourself. A lab is usually noisy and a little chaotic, so patience is a useful asset.

LABS

It is no new revelation that many students short-circuit the lab. Their goal of getting credit for each experiment motivates them to complete the mechanical requirements and derive an answer or a product within the time limit. That activity may, however, not lead to conceptualizing about the processes of science. Sometimes the logistics of the labs unintentionally further this gulf between mechanics and process. Some laboratory experiments so completely fill the two or three hour limit that students cannot get beyond the mechanics. Then conceptualizing is left as a voluntary, extra-curricular activity.

The link between the lectures and the lab may not be clear. Theoretically, the student should see the lab experiment as a test of principles presented in the lecture. If the principle is presented first in the lab, it should clearly relate to other parts of the course. Otherwise, the sequence may not mesh or the transfer may never occur in the student's mind. The senior professor may not appear in the lab and the lab instructors may not attend the lectures. So beginning students may perceive the lab as a separate course. Commonly, course exams include test questions from the laboratory experiment, but they are often separated from the other questions so the correlation is not required.

James Mathewson says, "The primary purpose of laboratories is not the presentation of ideas. That is the function of lectures. It is to give the students an intense personal experience with the stuff and operations of science. The worst kind of conventional lab, which we derisively call 'cookbook', fails most often because it is not exciting, challenging, or cogent."[1]

Many labs are a distortion because scientists don't have a recipe to follow when they are experimenting for real. They have to conceptualize before they work the mechanics, rather than the opposite. Students, supposedly, are providing or examining a principle in action after it has been explained by the professor. Here further problems arise because the set experiments in a lab may only deal with one variable while the principle has a universe of them. The whole approach of working with a factor or variable in an experiment determined by the lab instructor or professor is generally not nearly as exciting to the student as the designer anticipates. Many students would rather just believe the professor than test the principle. To these freshmen or sophomores the lab becomes a hurdle rather than an adventure.

Here are a few suggestions for improving labs:

1.   Get more personally involved.

   a.   Be visibly present in the lab each session, getting the puzzled feedback from the students and lending stature to the lab experience.

   b.   Work closely with the lab instructors. Many lab assistants feel they are relegated to an uncreative mechanical function. Their attitude may turn students off. But it can be a real motivating influence if the assistant is genuinely concerned. They need to help students perceive the process and not just the mechanics.

---

source unknown

[1]James A. Mathewson, "Student Laboratories: An Underdeveloped Education Resource", *Science Education*, Vol. 51, No. 2 (March, 1967), pp. 133-37.

2. Consider the open lab idea. Shift the set demonstration to the lecture—or to videotape—and challenge the students to design their own experiment to test the principle under consideration in the laboratory. Able students can go to work quickly. Many others will need a structure to help them design an experiment. Some will ask other professors for suggestions. Nonetheless, they will have to conceptualize, hypothesize, and design—not just follow directions. They will have to locate equipment much as scientists would in an original experiment. Lab assistants would become key consultants. Many projects would challenge or surpass their knowledge. This would be moving from drudgery toward excitement, but it would challenge the logistics of schedules, supplies, and even willingness of the staff. The open lab should be an option. To require it of everyone would be frustrating.

3. In a more traditional lab program, require the students to write a "think piece" after they have performed the experiment which conceptualizes the principle involved. Such an essay would ask students to explain the principle, suggest other ways to experiment with it, and extend the principle into other scientific or social consequences.

4. Assign the students to come to the lab with some thinking already done about the problem. Provide a case or problem and have students propose a tentative solution before the lab begins. Many lab hours are lost for freshmen and sophomores because they don't know how to proceed. They spin their wheels and get scared and depend on their neighbors. Often these students walk into the lab without knowing even the principle to be examined. They may walk out without knowing it either, even though they handed in a write-up.

TEACHING IN THE LABORATORY SETTING

Graduate assistants who are assigned to teaching responsibilities in laboratory settings have special responsibilities for planning, teaching, and evaluation. For those involved in science laboratory instruction, student safety is an important concern.

Science Laboratory Sections

PURPOSE OF LABORATORY SECTIONS

In most introductory science courses, laboratory sections are conducted in conjunction with lecture sessions to give the students an opportunity for hands-on experience with the scientific method. Generally, the lectures are conducted by professors, with GTAs responsible for conducting the laboratory sessions. In situations involving several laboratory sections for large lecture courses, a faculty supervisor may be assigned to oversee all teaching assistants. In other cases, GTAs may be assigned to assist specific professors. In any case, departmental expectations and procedures for laboratory courses are generally well established, and close contact between GTAs and their supervisors is essential to the realization of the department's objectives.

Laboratory sessions provide an excellent opportunity for students to acquire valuable technical skills and expand their understanding of the relation of scientific concepts and theories to "the real world." This practical experience is also intended to nurture the students' spirit of inquiry and to generate an appreciation of the nature of scientific discovery. To provide the extended time needed for the uninterrupted conduct of experiments, the lab sessions are usually longer and less frequent than regular class sessions, and students usually work individually or in small groups.

PLANNING FOR LABORATORY SAFETY

Laboratory sessions present a unique responsibility for student safety. The common safety precautions for laboratory operation may be second nature to the teacher, but the students are much less experienced and need close supervision, especially in the first weeks of the course. If improperly performed, simple procedures, such as inserting glass tubes into rubber stoppers or the decantation of toxic, volatile, or corrosive liquids, can produce serious injury. Consequently, to insure student safety, thorough instruction and frequent reminders of the necessary safety techniques must be primary objectives of every laboratory session.

If your assignment involves laboratory teaching, you should contact your faculty supervisor or departmental safety officer to obtain complete information about your responsibility for the safe conduct of your classes.

(1987) *Handbook for Graduate Teaching*. Office of Instructional Development, The Graduate School, University of Georgia.

ADDITIONAL RESPONSIBILITIES IN THE LABORATORY

Laboratory classes are often expensive for the department (because of space and equipment costs) and time consuming for the students. Although the teaching demands vary greatly among the laboratories in the various science disciplines, the following general suggestions may help new teaching assistants to provide for the effectiveness of laboratory sessions.

Learn all you can about the University's current safety regulations and procedures before classes begin. Be sure the first aid kit, fire extinguisher, and other safety equipment are accessible, properly labeled, and fully operable—and be sure you know how to use them. Review the basic rules for first aid and post in a conspicuous place the procedure for obtaining emergency assistance.

Check out the laboratory area and equipment so you can feel comfortable when classes begin. Become familiar with the laboratory stockroom so you will be able to locate extra supplies and equipment quickly if they are needed during a class session. Obtain a copy of the required student manual, review the supplies needed for the scheduled experiments, and notify the faculty supervisor if there are any shortages. Check with your supervisor regarding the availability of written materials, procedures and demonstration supplies (audiovisuals, slides, charts, and so forth) that you may need throughout the course.

THE FIRST DAY OF CLASS

As in other kinds of instruction, this is the time to set the tone for the rest of the quarter. Explain the importance of laboratory safety and make sure the students know what to do in the event of an emergency. Show them the laboratory facilities and give them a few minutes to become familiar with their surroundings. Then, explain in detail the general ground rules for the proper handling and storage of supplies and equipment. Emphasize that because the laboratory must be used by subsequent classes, work areas must be cleared and all equipment cleaned and stored before the end of each session.

Explain the relationship of the laboratory section to the overall course and point out that most of the experiments performed in introductory science courses are intended to illustrate basic ideas that underlie the fundamental concepts of science. Briefly review the types of experiments the students will be performing. Emphasize that because it will generally be necessary for you to present essential information and instructions at the beginning of each session they should be sure to arrive for class on time.

Identify the name and source of the manuals and supplies the students will be expected to purchase and explain the general type of preparation required for each session. Review the overall grading policy you will use and discuss your expectations regarding independent and collaborative work. Explain the types of notes and reports the students will be expected to prepare and, finally, make the assignment for the next laboratory session. If the work is to be done in pairs or small groups, it may be facilitative to arrange the groups at this time.

INSTRUCTION IN THE COURSE

Maintain student awareness of the educational importance of the laboratory experience by explaining the purpose of each experiment. Advance reading assignments or very brief introductory comments regarding the significance of an experiment may generate greater awareness of the nature of scientific research, and a few carefully selected study questions may help to focus student thinking. Unfortunately, laboratory experiments have occasionally been misperceived as irrelevant "busy-work," but proper student orientation and imaginative teaching can turn a laboratory exercise into an exciting and challenging learning experience.

Thorough teacher preparation is vital to each lab session. It is strongly recommended that you perform each assigned experiment, including the calculations and reporting that will later be expected of the students, before the laboratory session to determine if the instructions in the student manual are complete and clear and to be sure that the exercise can be performed in the time provided. This practice will also help you to discover those procedural difficulties the students are most likely to encounter. The theory on which the experiment is based should be reviewed in detail in preparation for responding to student questions regarding the theoretical significance and practical applicability of their newfound knowledge.

Because of the nature of laboratory instruction, it is very important to begin each session promptly. At the beginning of each session, demonstrate how the students should handle and care for any new supplies and equipment they will be using and review the essential safety precautions. Briefly but explicitly explain the purpose of the experiment, then give your students any necessary final instructions and let them get started. The introductory comments should be kept to a minimum to allow as much class time as possible for the experiment. Otherwise, the pressure of time may reduce a meaningful learning experience to an exercise in futility. In many cases, the instructions and the next class assignment can be written on the board before the session to greatly reduce the time needed for teacher comments.

During lab sessions you will have an opportunity for a unique involvement with student learning on a one-to-one basis. By circulating around the laboratory, you will be able to demonstrate your interest and accessibility to those students who may need help, while simultaneously monitoring laboratory safety. Care should be given to maintaining an informal manner while moving around the room. Regular pacing may be perceived as inspection tours; conversely, hovering in one place may be intimidating to the students in that area. Few teaching situations are as amenable as laboratory sessions to developing a personal rapport with students. So, with a little effort, you should be able to establish quickly an enjoyable working atmosphere.

At times, it may be tempting to take over and help a struggling student through a difficult part of an experiment, but this is generally inadvisable—except to avoid an impending problem. Students are generally more appreciative of assistance it if helps them discover solutions through their own resourcefulness. Questioning techniques are very effective for helping students redirect their thoughts and, if used skillfully, will generate creative thinking ability. So, if you can maintain your patience and diplomacy during your students' plodding efforts to learn by experimentation, teaching can be especially rewarding to both teacher and student.

Near the end of the class session, a brief summarizing discussion of the experimental results can be very productive. Allowing students to explain what transpired will help them to understand how to generalize from the experimental data to the concept under investigation. As the students discuss comparative variations in laboratory data, they may also gain additional insight into the nature of scientific knowledge and learn to appreciate their own abilities to apply experimental methods. The summary sessions will also provide you an opportunity to obtain group feedback regarding the lab procedures and practice.

Summary

Some of the points contained in this section are:

- Start the semester and each session formally and gradually loosen up. (p. 64)

- Don't use grades as a threat. (p. 64)

- Be thoroughly familiar with the procedures of the lab, the principles behind it and the relevance of the lab to the rest of the course. (p. 64)

- Strictly enforce lab safety rules. (p. 65)

- Frequent short quizzes may keep students prepared. (p. 65)

- Circulate around the room. (pp. 65, 70)

- The senior lecturer can lend stature to the lab experience by attending lab sessions. (p. 66)

- Consider the open lab idea. (p. 67)

- Have students write a "think piece" after the lab. (p. 67)

- Provide a case or problem beforehand and have students provide a tentative solution. (p. 67)

- Know where all the safety equipment is and how to use it. (p. 69)

- Thorough instruction and frequent reminders of the necessary safety techniques must be primary objectives of every laboratory session. (p. 68)

- Become familiar with the laboratory stockroom so you will be able to locate extra supplies and equipment quickly if they are needed during a class session. (p. 69)

- Perform each experiment, including calculations and reporting, before the lab session. (p. 70)

- A brief summarizing discussion of the experimental results can be very productive. (p. 70)

6
The First Class

It is 8:00 on a Monday evening early in September, and Mercedes is panicking.

"I can't do this. My first class is tomorrow morning. I feel sick. I think I have a fever. My legs are like rubber. Why did I ever accept this job in the first place?"

"Calm down; you're going to be fine. Everybody goes through this right before their first class," says Maureen. "It's normal to be nervous—but aren't you excited, too?"

"No! I'm just scared out of my wits!"

"Oh, come on, it's not as bad as all that," Steve says, "Lots of people teach and they all survive. My friend Alice had her first class today and she did fine. You will too."

"That's easy for you to say—you don't have to teach a lecture for weeks yet. All you have to do is lead a recitation section."

"What do you mean 'All I have to do'? That's tough, too, and I'm nervous about it. But I'm not going to let it get the best of me."

"Well, we'll see. . . " smiles Maureen. "Anyway, just be yourself. Don't be phony. Walk in, say, 'Hi, my name is X, and I'll be teaching this class this semester,' and take it from there. Believe me, it gets easier after the first couple of weeks. Even after a couple of years of teaching, I always get a little nervous before the first session of a new class: Will they like me? Is it a good group? Will the class be a good one? Everybody feels that way. Everybody who's any good, anyway."

Mercedes is not convinced. "But what do I have them call me? Mercedes? Miss Cruz? Prof. Cruz?"

"Well," Maureen says, "that's really up to you. You're really not a professor, but if you feel better with a more formal setting, then Miss Cruz is OK. If you don't mind some informality, try Mercedes. I always have them just call me Maureen; Ms. O'Reilly sounds funny to me."

"Yeah, I'm just going to have them call me Steve. But then I intend to be casual in class. I'm not real concerned about formality."

"I hadn't even *thought* about half of these things yet," moans Mercedes. "Oh, no. More to worry about. I'm going home to Venezuela."

"You're not going to do anything of the sort. You're going to go to class tomorrow and you're going to do just fine. You'll see. Tell you what. Meet us here tomorrow night and we'll celebrate your surviving the first class. Then we'll bug Steve about his."

Steve sighs. "Go ahead. I'm more worried about a class I'm taking. Stats. Yuck. I've always hated math and now I've got stats. My recitation will be a breeze compared to that."

THE FIRST DAY AND THE LAST DAY

The first day of class is important: "First impressions last." Some students seem to think the saying is "First impressions are the last"—they bolt out of their first-day recitation to the undergraduate office where they queue up to see what other section is open.

Your problem is to get over your first-day jitters and off to a good start. Instead of thinking of yourself as up for inspection, imagine yourself as the host of a party full of strangers, or the conductor of an amateur orchestra meeting for the first time: if you can make your students feel a part of something exciting and interesting, you'll have taken a big step toward ensuring the success of the next twelve weeks.

Let's hear how our physics T.A. handled the first day of his freshman section.

> "I was somewhat nervous and in need of a good beginning. Introducing myself, giving my office, phone number, and office hours was the ideal way to start. General course information with an explanation of homework and grading policy was useful to the students, and served as an "ice-breaker" for me.
>
> While doing this a paper was circulated to get names, majors, and any advance comments.
>
> Then to help assess the level of the students, I posed some mathematical problems which were essential to success in the homework: the law of cosines, common integrals, simple differential equations, changing coordinate systems. A second purpose was to get some frequently-used formulas into their notes that would save them from having to constantly repeat these calculations. The feedback was not the best, but by watching faces, I obtained a rough idea of what was new and what was familiar.
>
> I concluded by asking for questions and comments, and succeeded in getting a few to say what sort of section they wanted. Some wanted to go over homework, others wanted to see different problems, and still others wanted to rehash the lectures. At different times I endeavored to accommodate all of these views.
>
> As I see it now, the first day is important in getting off to a good start. The students get their first impression of the instructor and the better that is, the easier it will be for the teacher to reach his or her students."

That was a good first day, though not the only possible one. Let's amplify the account.

Heine, H., Richardson, P., Mattuck, A., Taylor, E., Brown, S., Olsen, A. and Russell, C. (1986). *The torch or the firehose? A guide to section teaching.* Massachusetts Institute of Technology.

The First Day

INTRODUCE YOURSELF

Your name, office, phone, office hours for sure. If you feel comfortable doing it, why not briefly tell your class something about yourself—your schooling, research, interests, and in general what you do besides teaching their class?

INTRODUCE THE CLASS TO EACH OTHER

To help students know who is in their section, make up a class list by passing around a paper on which they write their name, address, phone number, major (or possible major), and advisor's name. Circulate the list at the next couple of meetings as well, since some students try out different recitations at the beginning of the term. When it firms up, give everyone a copy.

Some students have suggested that they would like to hear the class members introduce themselves the first day. Of course this will take a while, and some may feel awkward about it. You could ask them if they'd like to do it. A relatively painless way might be to do it by living group ("Who here is from Baker House?") since students are interested in finding others who live near them to study with. (They'll tell you what the living groups are.) Instead of doing this the first day, you might wait with this until the second week when the class has stabilized, and the students are already beginning to recognize faces and voices and are getting curious about each other.

FIRST DAY SUBJECT MATTER

The main thing is to choose material which allows interaction. If the lecture hasn't met yet, you could quiz the class orally on background material. If the lecture has met, you could in addition ask them about the lecture or start in on the homework. If the lecturer isn't going to do it, you could outline the topics to be covered; you might give them some examples of what they'll be able to do by the end of the course, to whet their appetites. But avoid giving a long uninterrupted lecture: the message for today is that you want them to talk too.

LEARNING NAMES

There's magic in a name. Knowing your students' names will tell them you are interested in them as individuals, and will help interaction. Here are ways to learn names and in general get acquainted.

ID Picture

Students get some on registration day (though fall semester freshmen don't receive them until October). Ask for these pictures, and doctor them up as needed by inking in new mustaches, beards, glasses, longer hair (removing these poses more of a problem. . .)

Return Homework Individually

Call the students by their full name. If there isn't any homework, you could instead call the roll occasionally during the first few weeks. (Both of these let the students also see who's who.) As a further help, you can note down obvious physical characteristics, and where they sit, since for some obscure reason they usually stay in the same place all term. Note any unusually pronounced names; how you say their names is important to students.

Quick 5 or 10 Minute Quizzes

Discuss them right afterwards; you can use the results as part of the section grades, or just use them for diagnostic purposes. Go around the room while the students take the quiz and look at their names. This is a good way to see who needs help getting started -- offer it if it is needed.

Use the Names in Class

This is the fastest way to learn them. You can ask the students to give their names whenever they speak for the first week or two. Don't be inhibited by the fear of making mistakes; you'll be forgiven.

> I urge students to come in and visit during office hours in the first few weeks so that I'll get to see them as individuals instead of just as a sea of faces.
>
> –Math T.A.

In the lecture/recitation format, it's only the recitation teacher who has a chance to know the student. You'll be relied on in a variety of ways (completing evaluation forms, giving grades, talking to advisors, writing letters of recommendation, etc.) to provide information about your students. Students themselves will drop by for help and advice. The more you know about them, the more you'll be able to help. Treat getting to know them as an important business.

Don't be discouraged if the first day doesn't go as well as you had hoped. It's easy to exaggerate its importance. There's always the second day and all the others to come. Expect some quietness in the beginning as you and your students feel each other out. As you get to know each other, most of the first-day awkwardness will disappear and things will go more easily.

> Just keep coming to bat—once in a while you'll hit a home run.
>
> –Chem T.A.

The Last Day

Students get mired in the day-to-day details. A review on the last day gives you a chance to point out what's really important and how it all fits together—in other words, the Big Picture.

The simplest approach is to go back over the course outline, making comments—why we did this, where that topic leads, what we should have emphasized more at the time, and so on.

Or you may want to organize the material for them in a different way which sheds new light and makes it look fresh again. Pick something central to the course; if we wanted to understand just this, what else would we have had to study? Why did we study the topics in this particular order? If you had only one hour to give the essence of the course, what would you have taught? Three hours? Twelve? What's the thing you most regret having omitted? What will the students study in the sequel?

Or in a different vein, you could spend a while with them discussing the recitation or the course itself. In retrospect, what would have made the recitation more interesting? The course easier to learn?

Naturally, if there's a final, the students will want to know anything you can tell them about it. But don't spend the whole period on this. You might try to find out in advance what the lecturer will do the last day, and make your recitation complement that in some way.

It's been said that many a course is made by what happens on the last day. Don't just let your recitation stop: give it an ending.

MY FIRST CLASS

I'll never forget the first day of my first quiz section, I was very nervous. I couldn't sleep the entire weekend before. I couldn't think how to open the first day. How should I present myself? Being very short, I had visions of those towering freshmen not taking me seriously. Should I be very severe and set a martial tone for the entire quarter or should I walk in smiling and easy going? Should I wear a long skirt and pull my hair back or wear hot pants? I plotted my attack upon the lectern—should I stand behind it, beside it or in front of it? Did I want its authority to attach to me or did I want to be considered part of the group? I practiced roll call, passing out the reading list, the small preview of course material, and class dismissal.

On the Monday of the first day I got up at 6:30 a.m. and dressed very carefully—I decided to be myself and wear the hot pants outfit. I made a large breakfast, though by the time I was ready to eat, I couldn't. When I arrived, fear and anxiety were running wild through my body. My heart was thumping. Every surface I touched, I stuck to. And I shook. I watched the clock and counted off the seconds to 9 a.m. sharp. I didn't want to arrive early and have to stand there waiting for the buzzer.

9 a.m. I plodded into the classroom. The lights were dazzling. The electricity of the people sent my blood rushing faster. There were so many of them, all rustling papers. A hush fell as a I neared the lectern. It was so quiet I could hear my pulse in my ears. I reached the lectern and turned around. Forty eyes were focused on my body.

I blurted, "Hello. This is the first class I've ever taught, and I'm really nervous." The students sighed, slumped in their chairs and relaxed. And so did I.

Morrow, R. (1976). *What every TA should know.* In *The TA at UCLA: A handbook for teaching assistants. (1977-78).* The Regents of the University of California.

IN THE CLASSROOM
THAT FIRST CLASS:
"A FAREWELL TO LEGS"

"I spent ten minutes sitting on the can, oscillating with terror, before I steeled myself to go in there."

"At first, I felt super-confident, but when I got into the classroom—well, most of them looked older than me, all of them were BIGGER than me . . . I felt like jumping out of the window."

—English 109 TA

"The only way to atone for being occasionally a little overdressed is by being always absolutely over-educated."

—Oscar Wilde, "Phrases and Philosophies for the Use of the Young," *Chameleon*, 1894.

It should make you feel better to know that nobody actually expects you to *teach* anything at the first class. Think of it as a purely social event. Many teaching novices do find it helpful to treat the occasion as such, and spend the day before bemoaning the fact that they haven't a thing to wear. Your students may not care if you arrive clad in an Yves St. Laurent cocktail dress or a bathrobe, but don't count on it. These students are probably froshes, remember, and still on the threshold of learning to appreciate the primacy of Intellectual Beauty; one TA regretted having worn a pair of skintight jeans to her first class, since every time she turned to the blackboard, loud whispers could be heard from the male contingent in the back row which was, it seems, really "digging" her dorsal region.

Some TAs claim that arriving in the classroom early helps them to relax. By doing so, you can chat with the students as they come in, and convince yourself of their essential humanity. This is certainly less nerve-wracking than stumbling through the door ten minutes late to find yourself confronted with what appears to be a herd of TA-eating rogue elephants wearing U of W sweatshirts.

However you choose to make your entrance, once you are through the door the first thing to do, especially if your legs are buckling under you, is to sit down. Preferably on a vacant chair. Then introduce yourself, remembering to point out that you are their instructor, because unless you have decided to make your status unambiguous by donning your graduation gown, they could mistake you for just another, rather precocious, member of the class. Give the students your name, tell them what you are doing at the university—make something up if you don't know—and give them some relevant information about your background. You can then ask each member of the class to introduce himself or herself. You will have set the tone of these introductions; if you've just delivered a feverish monologue concerning the sexual proclivities of your cat Kevin, don't be surprised if they respond in kind. Likewise, merely informing them curtly of your I.D., OHIP and Social Insurance numbers will elicit introductions which resemble the rules governing POWs under the Geneva Convention.

Woodhead, J. (1979). *A manual for teaching assistants in the department of English.* Teaching Resource Office, University of Waterloo.

After the introductions, hand out and go over copies of the syllabus; tell them something about the course, the grading system and the assignments. Write on the blackboard your name, office number and hours and your extension number. Some TAs give their students their home telephone numbers in case of emergencies, and while your class is unlikely to abuse the privilege, some faculty members will warn you, perhaps from previous experiences, that the possibility cannot be completely ruled out.

During all these formalities, you should pass around the class a sheet of paper for them to write down for you their names, I.D. numbers, year, faculty and home telephone number. This last may be important if you have to cancel a class or chase up missing assignments.

If you have enough time, you could ask the students either to tell you, or write down for you, their reasons for enrolling in the course. In fact, many professors suggest that you do get the students writing in this first class. This first "assignment" is not usually graded, and it initiates the students into the practice of writing without their having to feel threatened or self-conscious by anticipating a grade.

Don't feel queasy about dismissing the class before the end of the period if their questions about the course seem to have been answered for the moment, and you run out of things to say to each other. Many TAs have to deal with the opposite problem; one had about thirty students in her class, and they never got past the introductions because they all became involved in recounting complete autobiographies; another had to evacuate the classroom the moment after she had said "Good afternoon," when one of the students dropped his lighted match into a polystyrene cup and set the desk on fire. "At least it broke the ice," quipped she.

COURSE MANAGEMENT

The following suggested patterns for course management will help you avoid some instructional pitfalls. They are paraphrased from, added to, and used with the permission of Walt Craig, professor and former ombudsman, Ohio State University.

- Be sure each student receives an up-to-date syllabus that covers the course. It should communicate clearly course objectives and your expectations of the student's performance. If the course has a mandatory pre- or corequisite, especially if there are no exceptions, place this requirement at the very beginning of the syllabus, underscored. If you ask students to drop your course for not having the appropriate prerequisite or for not attending the first class, make sure they understand their responsibility for dropping the course officially. If you or your department assume responsibility for dropping courses for students, be sure they understand that also.

- At the outset, give students an outline explaining the field they are going to cover. A first-day presentation to the class of an overall scheme of the course serves as an excellent orientation and lays the groundwork for all that follows.

- Describe and give the rationale for each requirement of the course and the weight each will have in the determination of the final grade. Discuss student responsibility in the course as you perceive it.

- If attendance is mandatory, indicate this early and discuss your rationale. Attendance policy should be made very clear, preferably in writing.

- Announce early, both orally and in writing, field trips and other special meetings. If these require activity on holidays and/or weekends, state this clearly. Suggest to the students that they discuss any course-time conflicts with other instructors as far in advance as possible. Be sure the departmental secretary has information on the time and place of all field trips in advance in order to fend questions better. It is imperative that your secretary know about any last-minute changes.

- Convey precisely, preferably in writing, your expectations for papers and projects. Discuss grading criteria, especially where evaluation will be based on non-specific guidelines. If possible, provide a sample paper for each student; if not, have some available in your office or in some other designated place for their perusal. Make students aware of the kind of help available to them in the Writing Lab.

- Have a definite written policy explaining your position on time extensions for paper and project completion.

- Include in your syllabus your understanding of what constitutes plagiarism, and discuss this in class.

Humphreys, L. and Wickersham, B. (1986). *A handbook of resources for new instructors at UTK.* Learning Research Center, University of Tennessee, Knoxville.

- Early in the course, present your grading criteria. Be sure this is thoroughly understood, for it can be a major interference with learning. The kinds of tests you give greatly influence how students study. Consider this carefully and then make a sample set of questions from the first study unit (perhaps ten multiple-choice and two essay, if this is your considered format). Attach these to your syllabus.

- If possible, have a system of early evaluative feedback for the students. Return tests and papers promptly with carefully noted suggestions. Try to keep your remarks in a positive and encouraging tone.

- Inform students of your examination schedule and your policy concerning make-up examinations. Remember that all good rules need built-in flexibility.

- If you have a university, department, or personal policy about incompletes, make this known. If you offer an "I" to a student, have a written document signed by both you and the student which states specifically the reason for the "I" grade and what will be required to complete the course, including any time limitation. A copy of the contract should be placed on file with the department in case you leave campus for any reason. This protects you and the student.

- Locate your office and mailbox for students. If you have an office phone, follow your department's policy on listing it. Definitely list your office hours in your syllabus. Encourage student conferences since they can prevent problems.

- Retain all your grading materials for review with students during the quarter and after final grades. Seeing the grading materials and hearing your rationale for the evaluation are important elements of a student's education. The test should be a valuable learning experience. Your evaluation MUST be defensible to both the student and a third party, should there be a dispute.

Summary

Some of the points contained in this section are:

- Stating your name, office number, office phone number, and office hours is a good way to start. (pp. 74, 80)

- Explaining homework and grading policies is a good ice breaker. (pp. 74, 80)

- Pass around a sheet of paper for students to list their names, addresses, phone numbers, ID numbers, major, etc. (pp. 74, 80)

- Allow opportunities for the class to get to know each other by letting them introduce themselves, or by sharing the above information. (pp. 75, 79)

- Choose the material for the first day that allows for interaction. (p. 75)

- Don't be discouraged if the first day doesn't go as well as planned. (p. 76)

- Arrive early to chat with students as they arrive. (p. 79)

- Don't feel queasy about dismissing the class early. (p. 80)

- Hand out a comprehensive syllabus. (p. 81)

- Have a written policy on time extensions, plagiarism, make-up exams, incompletes, etc. (pp. 81, 82)

- Discuss the rationale and weight of each requirement. (p. 81)

- Announce any special dates early in the course. (p. 81)

7
Teaching Tips

Late one afternoon, Steve finds Mercedes sitting in the back of her classroom.

"Trying to be both teacher and student? Isn't that just a little schizophrenic?" asks Steve with a grin.

"I'm just trying to imagine a student's perspective on this class and I thought sitting back here might help."

"That sounds reasonable. Are you ready to eat?"

"I'd really like to think some more about my class before we go. Do you mind?"

"Why don't you think out loud so I can, as always, solve your problem?" Steve asks with his usual charm.

"I don't really have a problem," answers Mercedes. "I think my class is going well. I'd just like some new ideas of things to do to make it even better. I don't mean hand out an evaluation sheet to the students: I've already done that. All I want is a little inspiration or encouragement, I guess."

"Feel like your teaching is in a rut, huh? Maureen has a folder of teaching ideas on her desk that I looked through last week. Some of the stuff in there assured me that I was doing the right things and I got some new ideas, too. Why don't you ask her if you can look at it?"

"Thanks. I will. Let's go over to her office now. Where are we eating, anyway?"

"We, my dear, are dining free of charge this evening."

"Uh-oh. I'm suspicious. What kind of crazy scheme have you dreamed up now?"

Steve looks shocked. "Moi? A crazy scheme? Is that any way to talk to the person who just solved your problem? Again?"

"I knew you'd bring that up."

"Of course. I always give myself credit, whether I deserve it or not. However, I have done some careful research and I have found that there are a half-dozen receptions for speakers, exhibit openings and so forth on campus tonight. I hope you like cheese and crackers."

SOME ROLES TEACHERS PLAY
(AND MOSTLY SHOULDN'T)

We cast you a little while ago as the tour leader for your recitation. Other roles that teachers play reflect how they feel about the course and their own place in it, and some have unfortunate consequences.

THE UNION ORGANIZER

It's tempting to ingratiate yourself with your section by telling them that it's not their fault they are having difficulties—they are victims of the System. You run down the book, the lecturer, the course in general. Of course any book or lecturer will occasionally be obscure, and it's all right to remark on it. But don't overdo this, because it can demoralize some of your students: why bother struggling if the cards are stacked against you?

THE LIFEBOAT CAPTAIN

Do you give your section the feeling of being tossed helplessly about on the seas of your course by Angry Implacable Lecturer-Administrator Gods? That's the effect of habitually using "they":

"I heard they are going to make the next problem set really tough."

"They are leaving infinite series out this year."

"I don't know if they will give you a thermo problem on the exam."

If this is the way you really feel, then there is too much of a gap between you and the lecturer for the good of the course and your students. There should be more staff meetings and you

Heine, H., Richardson, P., Mattuck, A., Taylor, E., Brown, S., Olsen, A. and Russell, C. (1986). *The torch or the firehose? A guide to section teaching.* Massachusetts Institute of Technology.

should be having more input on the problem sets and exams. In the meantime, at least compromise by staying on neutral ground verbally: "this was a difficult problem set," rather than "they made the problem set too difficult."

THE MAN WITH THE WHITE KID GLOVES

"The rest of this problem is just the usual algebraic garbage which I certainly don't intend to go through."

"That's just a standard $F = ma$ problem—doesn't anyone have something more interesting they want to ask about?"

Such remarks convey to your students that routine things are beneath you. Many of them will imitate your attitude, with disastrous results later on. The most common complaints from upperclass teachers are things like, "They can't even integrate dx/x," "Doesn't anyone teach them the periodic table any more?"

So let students know by your attitude that you consider such things important and that everyone must learn them well. Brief quizzes will reinforce this. Poorer students should concentrate particularly on this type of material; finding they know something well may encourage them to go further.

LEADER OF THE EXPEDITION

Every course has its winter of discontent—those times when most students are just struggling along and it seems as if they will never get to feel any mastery. It's up to you to cheer them on, to reassure them that others have made it and they can too, to hold up to them visions of the delights that await them on the summit. A little of your energy and enthusiasm supplied at the right moment can give them the lift that will take them the rest of the way.

TIPS ON TEACHING

Teaching is a highly individual activity. What is right for one TA may not work at all for another. Even so, there are some points that make life easier for all teachers. The tips here are not meant to be the last word on college teaching, but they have been helpful to many TAs at Cornell.

1. Try to know students personally. A "required" conference in the beginning of the term is a good way to get students into your office and gives them the chance to know that you're concerned about them. Being available to students in the classroom right before and after your class or lab will give them a chance to ask you questions when they need help most.

2. Look at your students when you talk. Try to attain eye contact with each student at least once during a class hour. In a lab, it's necessary to give each student individual attention. In a discussion group or lecture, that attention is just as important and looking directly at each student provides a good start. Remembering to look at each student individually will help you address the entire group. Often beginning teachers focus attention on one side or part of a class, usually those students who are most responsive initially. This excludes the rest of the group and makes those students feel less inclined than ever to talk in class.

3. Don't talk to the blackboard. This may sound silly—but there is a great tendency for teachers to look at the board while talking about the point or problem. The best rules for board use are:

    1. Write clearly and fairly large.

    2. Abbreviate only those words which are readily understood in abbreviated form.

    3. Don't erase before you have to.

    4. Write both the term and the definition for all unfamiliar vocabulary.

    5. Address the class—your voice won't carry if your back is turned to your audience.

4. Outline the day's schedule on the board. These may be the three or four points you are going to cover, or the different activities to be done in the class or lab. Students need to know where they're going; providing structure will tell them what they're expected to do and let them know you're organized.

5. Summarize the main points of each lecture, discussion group or lab section. The student should leave your class knowing exactly what he or she is expected to remember. The old adage of "tell them what you're going to say, say it, and tell them what you said" makes a lot of sense for an organized presentation of any kind.

Loheyde, K. (1978). *TA-ing at Cornell: A handbook for teaching assistants.* Office of Learning and Teaching Services, Cornell University.

6. Always plan your examples ahead of time. Many TAs run into trouble by making up a spur-of-the-moment example and not having it make sense. If you know that an example of wheat production in Russia would illustrate your point, figure out the details or the graph you could use in advance. Whenever possible, have the examples make real world sense or demonstrate factual information. That way students learn more from the example than the procedure involved in finding the solution to a problem.

7. Every TA wants to know how he or she is doing. One easy way to get information is to ask the students. After a week or two you may wish to have them anonymously respond to questions like: Are my directions clear? Can you hear me? Are points explained in enough (or too much) detail? Do you feel free to ask me questions?

    Some departments have their own questionnaires.

    Other ways to get feedback are to invite another TA or a friend in to observe your class, to invite the course leader in, to be videotaped to see how and what you do in front of the class.

CLASSROOM INTERACTION FORMATS

1. *Lecture with discussion.*

2. *Guided discussion about readings* (with or without study questions provided prior to assignment).

3. *Problem- or issue-centered task* for groups of 2-5 people (activity revolving around particular problem, question or exercise to deal with).

4. *Incident process* (using situation problems, requiring fact-finding and decisions for their resolution—can utilize small groups or large group). Variation is the *in-basket* technique where a specific problem or memo must be responded to by individual or small or large group.

5. *Case study method* (using report of a real situation—more complex than incident; group is to determine problem(s), significance of problem and probable solution(s); case study could be verbal or videotaped situation).

6. *Role play* can be an effective technique to apply, practice and problem-solve specific concepts and situations. Can be initiated by "trigger" case, film or tape. Other class members should have a role, such as critiquing the performance or trading places with the role players.

7. *Colloquy technique* requires moderator, 4-8 persons (3-4 representing class, 1-4 resource persons all on a panel); questions, problems and issues are raised by class representatives and responded to by resource group.

8. *Panel discussion* (3-6 persons discussing assigned topic—drawing from class members and/or outside resource people).

9. *Competitive panel technique* (3-6 people having an exploratory discussion on an assigned topic—these people may be challenged, ousted, and replaced by other class members; requires moderator).

10. *The expanding panel technique* employs a combination of presentation and discussion, consisting of a panel of 6-12 people as the nucleus. They activate the situation in a 15-30 minute exploratory discussion of a topic. Moderator guides and questions and comments. Then one at a time people join the group or whole class can join group.

11. *Symposium* is a series of related speeches by 2-5 persons on different phases of the same topic or closely related topics; speeches vary from 3-20 minutes and are followed up by questions/comments from audience directed at individual speakers.

12. *Debates* can revolve around a philosophical or complex question, or principles related to case study, incident, or problem. Other class members should have role as well—to assess arguments, vote (before and after), etc.

S. Jorgensen. (1987). *Instructional Resource Booklet for the Graduate Teaching Assistants.* The Center for Instructional Services. Old Dominion University.

13. *Interview technique* with guest speaker (5-30 minute presentation conducted before class or audience in which 1 or 2 resource persons respond to systematic questioning by an interviewer about a previously determined topic).

14. *Creative problem-solving group* for example, via a Synectics Approach using analogies and brainstorming activities followed by analysis and focusing of options generated. Groups probably work best with up to 15 people.

15. *Self-analysis exercises and questionnaires* to surface assumptions, preferences, characteristics, conceptions (and misconceptions).

NOTE: Any of these techniques, especially those involving problem-solving and debate, could be videotaped for the class to review and critique in light of the quality and effectiveness of the communication process.

44 THINGS TO DO IN CLASS

1. Hand out an informative, artistic, and user-friendly syllabus.

2. Direct students to a support unit for help on basic skills.

3. Tell students how much time they will need to study for this course.

4. Explain how to study for the kind of tests you give.

5. Put in writing a limited number of ground rules regarding absence, late work, testing procedures, grading, and general decorum, and maintain these.

6. Announce office hours frequently and hold them without fail.

7. Give sample test questions.

8. Give sample test question answers.

9. Explain the difference between legitimate collaboration and academic dishonesty; be clear when collaboration is wanted and when it is forbidden.

10. Give a pre-test of the day's topic.

11. Start the lecture with a puzzle, question, paradox, picture, or cartoon on slide or transparency to focus on the day's topic.

12. Use variety in methods of presentation every class meeting.

13. Stage a figurative "coffee break" about twenty minutes into the hour: tell an anecdote, invite students to put down pens and pencils, refer to a current event, shift media.

14. Incorporate community resources: plays, concerts, the State Fair, government agencies, businesses, the outdoors.

15. Show a film in a novel way; stop it for discussion, show a few frames only, anticipate ending, hand out a viewing or critique sheet, play and replay parts.

16. Share your philosophy of teaching with your students.

17. Form a student panel to present alternative views of the same concept.

18. Tell about your current research interests and how you got there from your own beginnings in the discipline.

19. Conduct idea-generating or brainstorming sessions to expand horizons.

Povlacs, J. (1986). 101 things you can do the first three weeks of class. *Teaching at UNL*, 8 (1). University of Nebraska-Lincoln.

20. Give students two passages of material containing alternative views to compare and contrast.

21. Distribute a list of the unsolved problems, dilemmas, or great questions in your discipline and invite students to claim one as their own to investigate.

22. Let your students see the enthusiasm you have for your subject and your love of learning.

23. Take students with you to hear guest speakers or special programs on campus.

24. Diagnose the students' prerequisite learning by a questionnaire or pre-test and give them feedback as soon as possible.

25. Hand out study questions or study guides.

26. Be redundant. Students should hear, read, or see key material at least three times.

27. Allow students to demonstrate progress in learning: summary quiz over the day's work, a written reaction to the day's material.

28. Use non-graded feedback to let students know how they are doing: post answers to ungraded quizzes and problem sets, exercises in class, oral feedback.

29. Use a light touch: smile, tell a good joke, break test anxiety with a sympathetic comment.

30. Organize. Give visible structure by posting the day's "menu" on chalkboard or overhead.

31. Use multiple media: overhead, slides, film, videotape, audiotape, models, sample material.

32. Use multiple examples, in multiple media, to illustrate key points and important concepts.

33. Make appointments with all students (individually or in small groups).

34. Tell students what they need to do to receive an "A" in your course.

35. Invite students to ask questions and wait for the response.

36. Probe student responses to questions and their comments.

37. Give students an opportunity to voice opinions about the subject matter.

38. Have students apply subject matter to solve real problems.

39. Grade quizzes and exercises in class as a learning tool.

40. Give students plenty of opportunity for practice before a major test.

41. Have students write questions on index cards to be collected and answered the next class period.

42. Learn names. Everyone makes an effort to learn at least a few names.

43. Find out about your students via questions on an index card.

44. Gather student feedback in the first three weeks of the semester to improve teaching and learning.

8
Objectives

One evening our three TAs meet for dinner at the local pizza place. After a brisk discussion of the football team, the conversation turns to (what else?) teaching.

"Well, Steve, how's your big lecture shaping up? It's only two weeks away, right?" asks Mercedes.

"Actually, it's fifteen days, seventeen hours, and thirty-two minutes away. Not that I'm counting."

"Sounds like he's nervous to me," Maureen grins to Mercedes.

"Well, I don't blame him. I'd be nervous about giving such an *important* lecture to that *huge* roomful of people, too," Mercedes grins back.

"Thanks, gang. You call this support?"

"Okay, okay, we're sorry. Sort of. Just tell us what the problem is, and we'll help," says Maureen.

"I know the material cold, and I'm not nervous about talking to a big group. It's just that I don't know what direction to take with the lecture. I'm not sure what to emphasize."

Maureen says, "That's where the objectives of the course can help out. If the course has specific objectives, and it should, those will tell you what the focus is and what the students are expected to know and do. Why don't you check the syllabus or ask your supervisor?"

Mercedes adds, "That's a good idea. I was a little lost at the beginning, too. I wasn't quite sure where my lectures were going. Then I talked with my department chair and we decided on the objectives for the course. After that it was much easier to plan my lectures."

"Sounds like a possibility," says Steve.

Just then, a roar erupts from a group of students at a nearby table. Steve walks over to find out what's going on. He comes back with a big smile as Maureen is dividing up the bill.

"What are you doing?" Steve asks her.

"Splitting the bill three ways, even though you ate half the pizza. What was all that uproar? And why are you smiling like that?"

"Three ways? No way! Dinner is on me. I just heard that the Red Sox clinched the division championship and I have a few dollars coming my way."

"That's terrific," says Maureen. "Go get us another pitcher."

IN THE CLASSROOM

After you have arranged the mechanics of the course and the advance preparation, you should concentrate on course objectives, lectures, and other devices to be used in communicating with students.

Course Objectives

It is important to understand and to communicate what you expect of students. Setting clear and appropriate objectives gives a focus to the course for both you and your students. For instance, a student might be expected to accomplish the following things as the result of having succeeded in certain classes:

> differentiate a polynomial function of one variable,
> conjugate a given verb in the future tense, or
> list and compare three different methods to prevent soil erosion.

These objectives are called *performance objectives*, and they have four characteristics.

1. they define goals in terms of what the *student* does, rather than what the instructor does;
2. they designate an *action* that the student performs to show attainment of the objective;
3. the action is applied to a specified set of *data*; and
4. they have clearly defined *criteria for success.*

Behavioral objectives such as these make it clear to students what they must do to succeed in the class and make it easier for an instructor to assign appropriate grades.

The objectives listed above are rather factual. A student either can or cannot perform each one. Behavioral objectives may also have judgmental elements, requiring decisions about *how well* a student performs a given task. For example, these are also appropriate performance objectives:

1. write a creative short story or piece of music,
2. choose one side of a controversial question and deliver a speech defending the validity of that position, or
3. design an experiment to test a given hypothesis.

For each of these, it is possible to say that a student did what was requested and did it at a particular level of quality.

Behavioral or performance objectives are distinct from *procedural goals*. These are goals and methods that you set for your class to facilitate your students' achieving a particular objective. You may want to challenge your students' ethical beliefs and cause them to reevaluate their positions, you may want to stimulate classroom discussion, or you may want to show students how a scientist approaches a problem. These are statements of what *you* as the instructor intend to do, probably to help the students accomplish certain learning objectives. After you

---

Humphreys, L. and Wickersham, B. (1986). *A handbook of resources for new instructors at UTK.* Learning Research Center, University of Tennessee, Knoxville.

have established the learning objectives for a course, work to select those teaching tools that promote student learning.

Learning objectives, then, reflect two important things to the student. First, what the student should be able to do as a result of the course, and second, how the student can demonstrate an ability to do that. Often objectives are stated as "understand the food chain" or "know about nuclear reactors." These statements do not communicate what type of learning students should pursue to accomplish the goals. How does one show s/he "understands" something? An alternative phrasing is "Be able to name the five stages in the food cycle, to explain what is transferred from each stage to the next, and to describe the effect of outside factors that inhibit or promote the transition from each stage to the next." Similarly, "Cover the material in chapters 1 through 10 of Greene's text" is not a precise objective for a student. Differentiate between an objective and a class activity.

Not all objectives need to be performance goals. In some classes we may want to expose students to a value structure different from their own, we might want them to observe a kindergarten class under the leadership of a Montessori teacher, or we might expect them to develop an appreciation for a good painting, mathematical proof, or football play. These are, however, things which are difficult, if not impossible, to evaluate on a test. This is not to imply that these are not important goals for a class. Quite the contrary, they may be the most important goals in some classes. The point is that since it is hard to measure them in any meaningful way, it is difficult to incorporate them into a course grade. They are perfectly valid things to want to accomplish in a class, but they are inappropriate to include in a student's grade.

The nature and balance of lecturing, questioning students, discussions, testing, and grading in a given class should be determined in relation to the objectives set by the instructor and, in some cases, by the department. In both formal and informal ways, students should be able to demonstrate that they have mastered certain skills and competencies and have met the objectives of a course. For example, if we are going to ask students to analyze, synthesize, and evaluate materials, the occasion must be there to do this, not only on examinations but during class discussions.

SAMPLE OBJECTIVES

The learner will be able to name the components of transistors without error, given appropriate diagrams and visuals.

The learner will be able to add, subtract, multiply and divide pairs of two-digit numbers without error.

The learner will be able to identify slides of cells as normal or cancerous with 100% accuracy.

The learner will be able to make an amaretto chocolate fudge cheesecake consistent with the guidelines set out in Julia Child's fourth edition, given the appropriate ingredients and equipment, in one day's time.

The graduate student will be able to identify the sleeping undergrads from the non-sleeping undergrads in his/her recitation section with 85% accuracy.

The graduate students will be able to name at least five of the ten establishments that are on the Ten Best Places for Happy Hour list, given 10 minutes.

Given a dictionary and a reference book on writing style, the learners will be able to compose a 500 word essay on the topic of their choice, with no more than four grammatical errors, in two hours.

The learner will be able to correctly solve 10 out of 12 quadratic equations, within 30 minutes, using the procedure taught in class.

Summary

Some of the points contained in this section are:

- Setting clear and appropriate objectives gives a focus to the course for both you and the students. (p. 96)

- Performance objectives are stated in terms of what *action* the *student* will perform with which *data* and to what *criterion of success.* (p. 96)

- After you have established learning objectives, select the teaching tools that will help students achieve the objectives. (p. 97)

- Learning objectives tell the student what they should be able to do and how they can demonstrate that ability. (p. 97)

- Not all objectives need to be performance goals. (p. 97)

9
Media

Maureen drops by Steve's office one morning to find him working on some drawings.

"Hi. What're you doing?" she asks.

"Oh, making some overheads for my recitation tomorrow," he says. "We're discussing the deliberations over the framing of the Constitution, and sometimes it helps to see things to get discussion started. When I finish with these, I'll run them through the copy machine and make transparencies from them."

"Gee, I didn't know you could make transparencies that way. I've never used overheads; they always looked too hard. Professors are always screwing them up—you know—getting things upside down, backwards. Too much hassle for me: I just use the blackboard."

"Blackboards are easy and boring. Everybody uses blackboards. And it's not that hard to use overheads. If you've got some material that could be presented visually, it's usually easy to do it. If I ever get a class of my own, I want to use films and videotapes and things like that. It spices up the class and breaks the monotony of lecturing with blackboards."

"Hey, it's not so easy to use blackboards, you know. How many times have you seen some poor soul scribbling indecipherables on a board and muttering to the wall so in the end no one knows what's going on? It's a skill."

"I suppose so. But try using something else sometime. Who knows—you might even like it. Turns out that I can be of some help, too, huh? I'm giving *you* advice now."

"Don't let it go to your head. We'll see how it works first. You want to grab some lunch?"

"Sure. Your treat?"

"Dream on, kiddo. Dream on."

THE EFFECTIVE USE OF MEDIA

Let's assume you are teaching a 50 minute class in whatever your subject happens to be. Let's assume that for about half the period you'll be encouraging and answering questions, and having discussion in class. So that for, say, 20 minutes you are lecturing, laying it on your students.

Assuming you utter 150 words per minute (which is slow) you are using at least 2000 words.

How many vital ideas and concepts are you transmitting (or concealing) in those 2000 words? That will vary, of course, but presumably it will be five or ten or fifteen ideas per class. How many of these do you really expect your willing students to remember and be able to use properly? Even though they will be repeated and reinforced in textbook and class discussion?

This is the key reason for using media: to lay out concepts and ideas graphically, and to show how they relate with each other, will help your students to organize them in their minds and so to recall them more easily.

It's like making a map of new territory you are going to explore—you can study the different places and areas and SEE how they sit in regard to each other and just how they are connected together.

The belief that visualizing ideas locks things in the memory is as old as the Greeks and Romans, who taught public speakers to form mental landscapes for each situation and attach key words to prominent features of the picture in the mind. It is as new as the latest psychological theories about one-half of the brain being used for *verbal*, and the other half for *spatial* perception. By combining the two you will be helping your students use both sides of their brains.

Visuals and symbols help explain scientific formulae, themes in literature of the kinships of the Kwakitul. You do not have to be Raphael or Picasso—simple blocks and triangles and circles and arrows can be very potent. With a little practice you will find yourself adding stick figures and other symbols. You can start by copying characters from some favorite comic strip.

For visuals you can make yourself in class using blackboard or overhead projector:

1. Practice sketching them and revising on scrap paper beforehand, till you arrive at the best lay-out. Show you sketches to friends for their opinions on clarity and effectiveness.
2. Don't be afraid to draw them large—most beginners tend to start with visuals that are too small.
3. Start your in-class drawing at the most important point, rather than in one corner, for research shows that the point you start at is the place best remembered. For more complicated visuals, you will want to prepare them ahead of time on transparencies or slides—and for these media you can also copy materials from all sorts of sources.

Cohn, C. and Buckley, J. (1977). *A TA's guide to Syracuse University.* Syracuse University.

SEEING IS UNDERSTANDING: USING THE BLACKBOARD

Science and engineering teachers almost always have to write things down—the diagrams, the formulas, the derivations. Yet their blackboard often seems to be more a record of their stream of consciousness than anything else.

The reason you're going to fuss over making the board look good is that you know that at any moment

• Half your students aren't listening—they're woolgathering;

• Half your students aren't understanding—they're just taking notes. (The two halves might overlap some.)

You want the board to tell what went on well enough so that the daydreamers won't be lost when they tune in again, and so the baffled can use their notes to figure things out later (maybe with their roommate's help).

Neatness Counts

The basic rule is: don't skip around the board, tucking in formulas wherever there's a little space; use the board sections in an orderly way. One good method is to start at the extreme left panel, go down, continue with the next panel to its right, and start over at the left again when the entire board is full. The writing itself should be clear, the right size (easily read but not wasting a lot of space), and written level. Check these things occasionally after class by looking at the board from the rear of the classroom.

My chem T.A. draws all the structural formulas in the air with his fingers. He must think chalk is one of the rare earths.

Write It and Leave It

Write down enough (including the statement of the problem for the sake of those who didn't bring their books or notes to class) so things can be figured out later; standard abbreviations will help to save space. Don't erase until all the boards are filled, and don't simplify expressions by using the eraser, as this drives note-takers up the wall. Put important things in boxes to emphasize them visually, or use colored chalk.

Heine, H., Richardson, P., Mattuck, A., Taylor, E., Brown, S., Olsen, A. and Russell, C. (1986). *The torch or the firehose? A guide to section teaching.* Massachusetts Institute of Technology.

A FEW MORE SUGGESTIONS ON BLACKBOARD USE

- Practice drawing pictures or diagrams ahead of time, if you have trouble with them.

- Pull the shades if there is sunlight or glare on the board—even your best students would rather squint than tell you.

- Your chalk squeaks? Watch out for this since it is something that usually annoys the class much more than the teacher. Just break it in half, and hold it at a 45 degree angle to the board.

- Try to stay inside the squares, that is, don't write across the vertical cracks of the blackboard if you can help it. It can be rather confusing visually (also, the bears might get you).

- If you see your students' heads waving back and forth, it means they can't see what's written on the bottom third of the board. Don't use this part. Compensate by writing the top line higher up: stand on tiptoe if you have to. (It might also mean they can't see through you—standing in front of what they write is a method many teachers use to cover the material.)

> **Aim not to cover the material, but to uncover part of it.**
> **–quoted in "You and Your Students"**

Other Visual Aids

Occasionally using other aids besides the blackboard can lend some variety and excitement to the recitation—just the feeling that you've gone to a little trouble on their behalf can mean a lot to your students and to the general atmosphere.

The overhead projector can show complicated tables and diagrams, photographs of famous people in the field, and pretty commercial color transparencies with successive overlays that add information. It lets you face the class, and you can refer back to earlier points easily. On the negative side, the material disappears from view rather quickly and in the wrong hands things can be soporific.

Slides and film strips might be other possibilities. Your department may have models lying around, or working equipment that can be shown. See the course head, the departmental undergraduate office, or the lecture-preparation staff to find out what's available that can be used.

OVERHEAD TRANSPARENCIES

DEFINITION

An *overhead transparency* is an image on clear acetate or plastic which has been prepared for use on an overhead projector. The acetate is usually eight and one-half inches by eleven inches to fit the stage of most overhead projectors. An *overhead projector* is a device which projects the image on a screen. It is placed on an art or tabletop in front of an audience. It may be used in a completely lighted or semidarkened room. Projectors are not expensive. Classroom models cost $150 to $275.

CHARACTERISTICS

Overhead projection is a widely used medium of instruction. It is a simple and effective means of communication that enables you to interact with your class. The lens system of the overhead projector is designed to allow placement of the projector in the front of a room so that you can face the class when using it. This projection angle often causes the rectangular image to appear in a trapezoid form (called keystoning; see Figure 11.1). Keystoning is corrected by moving the bottom of the screen slightly away from the projector, as shown in Figure 11.2. The projector should be placed as low as possible so that the body of the equipment does not interfere with the line of vision between the students and the screen.

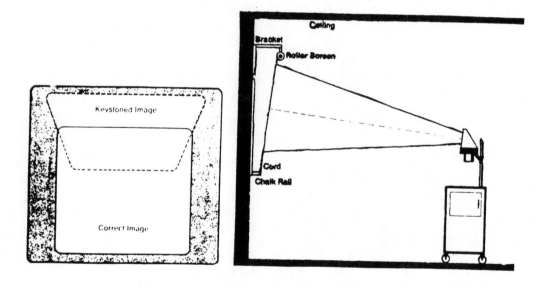

Figure 11.1   Figure 11.2

Some overhead projectors have attachments for rolls of acetate. Rolls permit you to prepare a number of different items to be projected; then you merely roll one after the other onto the stage, as you need them. The roll cuts down on the distraction caused by constantly changing transparencies. It serves as a projected "chalkboard."

Gerlach, V. and Ely, D. (1980). *Teaching and media: A systematic approach.* (2nd edition). NJ: Prentice-Hall.

Transparencies are not the only materials that can be used on the overhead projector. Opaque objects placed on the stage of the overhead projector will project as silhouettes and can be used effectively to demonstrate relative sizes and shapes of objects. Transparent or translucent objects can be placed on the stage. For example, water in a shallow glass container can be moved in such a manner that the wave action is projected on the screen.

There are tools you can use for writing or drawing on acetate when creating overhead transparencies. These include:

Felt Markers
These are convenient and inexpensive. Permanent ink markers create the boldest images and are useful when you plan to use a transparency over a long period of time. Water-soluble markers do not produce as dark an image, but the lines are easily erased with a damp cloth from the acetate sheet as new information is added.

Colored Pencils
These are inexpensive and often erasable with cloth and water. However, colors usually do not project accurately. Be careful to project a sample of colors you intend to use before creating an overhead transparency. A brown-colored pencil, for example, can produce a gray image on the screen as light passes through it. Some colored pencils have opaque lead; regardless of the color of the line, it will appear black on the screen.

India Ink
This creates the most solid lines but is not easy to work with. Black is an efficient color for overhead projectors; colored inks do not work quite as well.

Typewriting
Most typewriter type is too small to project letters of adequate image size. However, typewriters with *bulletin* or *primary* type (usually available in school libraries) produce letters large enough to be seen by a class of normal size.

Other Methods
Most graphic supply stores have stick-on, dry transfer, and opaque letters and symbols that can be used to create overhead transparencies.

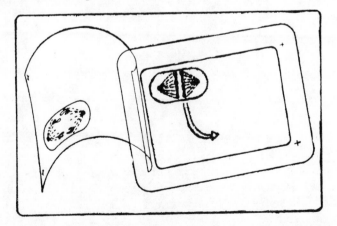

Two effective methods of presenting information with an overhead projector are *disclosure* and the use of *overlays*. Disclosure is the process whereby you progressively reveal the various elements of your transparency to the audience. This is a particularly useful method when you are explaining steps in a process or when the transparency presents too much information to be easily comprehended at once. Any opaque material, such as a file folder or a sheet of paper, can be used to cover parts of the transparency until ready for projection.

Overlays refer to additional images, colors, or words which are *added* to the transparency's base visual. Overlays usually are additional sheets of acetate that are hinged onto the base transparency frame with a piece of tape. When you are ready to present additional information, you simply flip the overlay transparency atop your base visual. One overlay or several can be added, usually up to four, with projector remaining clear. It is a good idea to number your overlays to insure the correct sequence when you use them.

Summary

Some of the points contained in this section are:

- The key reason for using media is to lay out concepts and ideas graphically and to show how they relate with each other. This will help the students to organize the ideas in their minds and recall them more easily. (p. 102)

- Practice sketching visuals large enough to be seen from the back of the room. (p. 102)

- Be neat and organized in the way you put information on the board. (p. 103)

- Write it and leave it; don't erase until the board is full. (p. 103)

- Be on the alert for glare (pull shades) and for squeaky chalk (break it in half). (p. 104)

- Don't block the board from view. (p. 104)

- When using the overhead, correct keystoning by moving the bottom of the screen away from the projector. (p. 106)

- Try using "disclosure" or "overlays" on the overhead. (p. 107, 108)

10
Self-Evaluation

In early October, Maureen and Mercedes go to a movie. To neither's surprise, they talk about teaching on the way to the theater.

"You know what my big problem is?" asks Mercedes. "Knowing how well I'm doing. It's very hard for me to tell whether I'm getting across the material and how well I'm doing it. The students' assignments are pretty good, but I'm very uneasy about my performance so far."

"Well, from everything you've told me, it sounds like you're doing great. But would you like something more formal? Like an evaluation?"

"I guess so, but I'm a little scared of that. What if I'm no good?"

"Well, it doesn't have to be scary. There are lots of ways to evaluate yourself. Ask your students what they think. Stop class 10 minutes early and ask them. Pass out evaluation questionnaires. Have your faculty supervisor sit in. Have Steve and I sit in. That might be kind of fun."

"Not a bad idea. Have you ever done anything like that?"

"We're evaluated all the time in the English department. They've got to—we've got so many students and so many instructors that they need to know how we're doing pretty regularly. Actually, a couple of friends of mine, Tracey and Eric, sit in on each other's classes at least once a semester. It's tough sometimes, but worth it. I'd love to sit in on your class if you wouldn't mind."

"Mind? I'd love it. How about Wednesday?"

"Sure. Should I ask Steve? I think he's free."

"Oh, why not. What can he say about me that he hasn't already said about his stat professor?"

EVALUATION BY STUDENTS

A topic related to your evaluation of students is the students' evaluation of you and your class. Just as your exams are used as motivators for students and to enable them to assess their mastery of certain material, you can use student evaluations to provide information on the conduct of your class. Some departments provide their own questionnaires, or you may want to create your own. Here are some tips on student evaluation of instruction.

- Consider scheduling an evaluation early—before the middle of the term. In this way, you have the results back in time for them to affect how you complete the term. Students will feel more willing to share their suggestions if they can see it will help the class they are still taking. On the other hand, your department may prefer to administer questionnaires near the end of the quarter, and to assure the students that grades will be determined long before the responses are returned (anonymously) to the instructor. If this is the case, you may want to administer you own questionnaire earlier and the departmental one at the end of the quarter.

- Ask students about things they are able to answer. Students are in an excellent position to comment on your speaking voice, the legibility of your writing, your consideration in dealing with student feelings, the clarity of your objectives, and your apparent preparedness for class. They are less qualified to evaluate the appropriateness of your objectives, the logic to the order of your material, or your ability to fit this subject into a broader field of knowledge.

- If you have a small number of questions (for example, five) that would help you shape your teaching throughout the quarter, distribute these for quick responses some day. Use the feedback to concentrate on improving one aspect of your teaching at a time.

- Invite a friend or trusted colleague to sit in and observe your class, preferably for several sessions, and share with you comments on your teaching. Return the favor in the other person's class.

Humphreys, L. and Wickersham, B. (1986). *A handbook of resources for new instructors at UTK.* Learning Research Center, University of Tennessee, Knoxville.

HOW WELL DO YOU TEACH?
"BIG BROTHER IS WATCHING YOU"

The most immediate measure of your teaching abilities is your students' response in class: if they start doodling frantically, yawning or talking among themselves, if their numbers dwindle noticeably as the term progresses, if you are distracted from your grand orations by the sound of snoring, if skirmishes and scuffles break out among your students at the beginning of class over who is going to occupy the back two rows of seats—you *may* be justified in suspecting that your presence is not as compelling and charismatic as you have believed. On the other hand, sleeping, snoring, absenteeism and scuffling seem to be a way of life among many undergraduates, and are not necessarily any reflection on your abilities as a teacher. If you do feel that you are doing something very wrong, the way to find out for certain is to invite a disinterested observer to one of your classes.

Another TA
A fellow teaching assistant is the least threatening and least obtrusive observer. Your students are unlikely to notice him or her and will behave more naturally than if they are aware of an academic Big Brother sitting in the corner. The TA may afterwards be able to point out to you any basic flaws in your teaching such as speaking too softly, asking the wrong kinds of questions or using the wrong kinds of material.

Woodhead, J. (1979). *A manual for teaching assistants in the department of English.* Teaching Resource Office, University of Waterloo.

THE PROFESSOR IN CHARGE OF THE COURSE

The professor in charge of your course will almost certainly want to visit one of your classes at some point during the term to assure himself or herself that you are not doing anything horribly unethical or inappropriate such as administering corporal punishment to your students. He or she will remain as inconspicuous as a professor is able by sitting quietly at the back of the classroom, and will not interfere unasked with the conduct of the class, unless a student proceeds to inflict grievous bodily harm upon your person, in the event of which he or she will rally the students to your aid.

It is a good idea to inform your students a week in advance of the professor's visit, and make it clear that they are not "on trial;" if anybody is, you are. After the class, the professor will discuss with you his or her estimation of your "performance," and perhaps make some suggestions that would improve your teaching.

Woodhead, J. (1979). *A manual for teaching assistants in the department of English.* Teaching Resource Office, University of Waterloo.

THE MOST FASCINATING SHOW ON EARTH: HAVING YOUR CLASS VIDEOTAPED

If you have the overwhelming desire to see yourself on the silver screen, or, at least, to observe your classroom demeanor for yourself, arrange to have one of your classes videotaped. You can watch the resulting feature in private, or you can haul in some fellow TAs clutching boxes of popcorn to help conduct a critical post-mortem on your performance.

This procedure has its obvious benefits, as well as its disadvantages: a sudden confrontation with your facial contortions, nervous tics and habit of flailing your arms around wildly when talking to a roomful of people may be disconcerting and could make you a self-conscious paranoid for the rest of your life. On the other hand, many teachers may find such revelations a useful step towards self-improvement.

It is up to you to decide whether or not you inform your students that they are about to become film stars, since it is possible to conduct the class in a special room where the camera is hidden behind a two-way mirror. They may, however, be suspicious of this change in surroundings, and rather than fabricate some story about the ceiling of your usual classroom having a leak in it, it may be as well to let them know exactly what is going on—at the risk of their turning up to class dressed in tuxedoes and Christian Dior creations, adopting their best CBC accents and spending the whole session waving, posing and making mouths at the camera.

Woodhead, J. (1979). *A manual for teaching assistants in the department of English*. Teaching Resource Office, University of Waterloo.

Summary

Some of the points contained in this section are:

- Evaluate early in the semester. (p. 112)

- Ask someone you trust to sit in on your class. (pp. 112, 113)

- Ask questions the students can answer; your speaking voice, preparedness, presentation, not about the appropriateness of your objectives. (p. 112)

- Have yourself videotaped and watch the playback. (p. 115)

11

Evaluation of Students/Grading/Test Construction

It is about 7:00 one late October evening. Mercedes comes into Rosemary's Place and sits down with Maureen and Steve. She is not happy.

"Thanks a lot." she says, disgusted.

"What's wrong?" Maureen asks.

"I followed all of your advice last week about that exam I had to write for my class. I did everything you said to do. I made sure the questions made sense, that they tested the things we had discussed in class, that they were the right type of questions for the subject matter, and I wrote great instructions. I did everything right. And *still* I had a student complaining about it."

"What did she say?" asks Steve.

"It was a he," she answers. "He didn't do very well, and he said that the test was unfair and that I hadn't prepared the class for it. I think I did. We covered all that material and I even held a review session the class before the exam. He also said that I made a mistake grading his paper. There's no way to win."

"How did you grade them?" Maureen asks gently.

"I did just as you said: I graded each question individually and I didn't look at anybody's name. Oh, this makes me so mad!"

"Calm down, it's going to be OK," says Maureen. "Even though you do everything right, there's bound to be someone who complains. And don't hit me, but there's also the possibility that he's right about your grading."

"What?!"

"Take it easy. It's very hard to admit that you've made a mistake, but it's even harder when it's an exam or a paper grade. Look over the paper again, or have someone else in the department have a look at it. Try to be fair, and if you find out you goofed, admit to it, say you're sorry, and change the grade. That's really the only fair thing to do."

"I guess so. I tried so hard to do everything right, and look what it got me."

"Forget it," says Steve. "If only one student complained, you did fine. Order some french fries and you'll feel better."

"You mean *you'll* feel better," Mercedes replies. "Every time I order french fries, you eat most of them."

"I'm a growing boy," Steve protests.

"Yeah, growing all the time," says Maureen. "Too many french fries."

"Funny. You should be in a book or something."

"Oh, I will be someday," sighs Maureen.

EVALUATING YOUR STUDENTS: ASSIGNMENTS, EXAMS, GRADES

ASSIGNMENTS

In a system where courses compete with each other for the student's time, those without regular assignments and clear expectations will lose out. Students in them get so far behind they can no longer even ask questions, let alone follow what is new.

Students tend to gauge their understanding by how well they can do the assignments, so these should be set carefully. This is usually done centrally; your job as recitation teacher will be to help your students with the homework, smoothing over some of the difficulties without robbing them of all exertion. If there's a weekly problem set, look it over as soon as it comes out and keep it in mind when planning what problems to work in class, but don't sabotage it by working essentially identical problems! (Baby chicks should not be helped out of the shell.)

Daily assignments, handed back at the next recitation, probably are best of all. They give you and the students steady feedback, your students get used to regular study and stay up-to-date, you get to know them better, the recitation is livelier, and the course more exciting. Sometimes the work is reduced by grading just one problem carefully and checking the physical existence of the others, but this can produce frustrated students. How about just giving one problem?

> It would be nice if recitation instructors graded all of our homework. If we didn't happen to get the one problem they graded, it was like we didn't even do the homework at all (in terms of the grade).

In most courses, homework isn't counted too heavily in the final grade, since students work with each other on it. It should certainly make a difference in borderline cases (there are often a lot of these), and in letting students who choke on exams still pass the course.

The most important thing about correcting the assignments is to do it promptly—which means handing them back at the next recitation after they come in. You're going to grade them sooner or later, after all; doing it sooner means that the students get the papers back while the work is still relatively fresh in their minds. You can then discuss common difficulties in the recitation, and the material still will be current in the course. It's also important for morale—it gives students the feeling that you are interested in their work and take them seriously, and they in turn will respond by putting effort into your recitation.

EXAMINATIONS

Students take exams very seriously, which means that regardless of what you think of tests as teaching devices or as tools for evaluation, you have to take them seriously also.

Heine, H., Richardson, P., Mattuck, A., Taylor, E., Brown, S., Olsen, A. and Russell, C. (1986). *The torch or the firehose? A guide to section teaching.* Massachusetts Institute of Technology.

REVIEW SESSIONS

At the last meeting before an exam, your students will hope for a review. Giving a good review session means a little work in the preparation, but you'll be rewarded by the feeling that they are hanging on your every word. You might at long last get some questions.

For a *quiz review*, usually the class hour is divided up: a brief outline of what the quiz will cover (very brief if it was done in lecture), comments and hints about those parts of the material which you feel are most likely to give them trouble, a question period, and finally working sample problems from old exams if there is time.

Exams tend to fall into routine patterns, and you or your students may be lucky and score a direct hit during the quiz review. They'll love you for it, but after the elation has worn off you may feel some qualms. Try for near misses instead. Remember that your overall purpose is to review a section of the course and help them see things in perspective, not just teach them how to pass the exam.

GRADING THE EXAM

This is often done by the entire course staff together, or at least the course head supplies detailed instructions. If not, you'll have to use your own judgment. If this is your first time as a section teacher, especially if you come from abroad, talk to some of the experienced section teachers to get a feeling for the standards—show them a few of your graded papers, or ask to see theirs.

Look over some of the papers to see what the common mistakes are, and decide in advance on the partial credit you will allow for them. It is fairer to grade one problem at a time, shuffling the papers between problems.

Everything said about grading homework on time applies with even greater force to the quizzes.

HANDING BACK THE PAPERS

Your students will want to know at least the section averages: some teachers also give a histogram which may be so detailed that every grade is actually listed. Some give no information at all, hoping to downplay competition, but of course the students can find out other section averages, and it's silly to make them struggle for the information. Much depends on your manner and on course policy.

There also should be solution sheets. Discuss common mistakes, as everyone can learn from others' mistakes, but keep it interactive: "What's wrong with this . . . ?" It's also interesting to present unusual or elegant methods that appeared on some papers. (This goes for problem sets as well.)

THE BAD EXAM

It happens all the time. The exam was too long or too hard—your section average was 42 and your students sit there stunned. They've never gotten such low grades in their life.

Or the average was 65, but there was a trickily worded question that misled half your students, who feel they could have gotten 20 more points if it had been worded as it was in the homework.

The average was 92, and the students who have been walking on air all weekend because they felt they did so well have suddenly fallen to earth. "If everybody's somebody, then no one's anybody."

All you can do is reassure, offer sympathy, tell them it's not an uncommon occurrence. Even if you are as angry as they are, you shouldn't play union organizer: "This exam could have been better," not "They really goofed on this one".

How does it happen? The lecturer or course head may be inexperienced at making up exams, he or she may not have had enough contact with the problem sets, they may have worked so long over the exam that it seemed easy at the end, etc., etc. For sure, it wasn't pretested. Ask that future exams be taken in advance by two recitation instructors, to judge the length and difficulty and spot poor questions. Volunteer yourself (you'll have to work out the exam later anyway.) You should be able to write down the answers to an hour exam in ten to twenty minutes depending on the field.

FINAL GRADES

Lecture-recitation courses should have a uniform grading policy: how much each exam and the homework (and class quizzes and labs) will count. Student grades often are assigned in a meeting of all section instructors. You will usually have some leeway, however, and should take subjective considerations into account—giving a higher grade to the student who has steadily improved, for instance, even though the numerical total is the same as another who has steadily declined. Regularity and performance on assignments and brief quizzes can be used to raise or lower grades near the boundaries.

ALTERNATE TYPES OF ASSIGNMENTS

Writing activities don't have to be lengthy papers: they can be brief exercises spanning a sentence to several paragraphs. Written assignments do not have to be graded. They could be part of a larger, progressively more complex assignment. Fellow students could participate in critiquing each others' assignments, followed by opportunities for re-writes. Examples of written assignments might involve:

1. Analyses of data, problems or cases, including analysis of problems and contributing factors, as well as positing alternative paths, solutions or consequences;
2. Formulating questions or hypotheses, given specific facts or information;
3. Writing paragraphs that meaningfully and accurately interrelate a group of vocabulary words;
4. Writing observations, journals or reports of activities and projects;
5. Comparing or critiquing data, readings, performances, videotapes/films, experiments, etc.; and
6. Translating theories or principles into hypothetical, concrete applications.

Writing assignments can complement other types of assignments. Besides thinking in terms of diverse writing assignments, various disciplines could consider a broader range of inquiry and expressive assignments, as well.

1. Inquiry projects entail small mini-research projects as well as larger research/interview/survey activities—either as individual or team responsibilities.

2. "Expressive products" represent performances or creative designs. Students could be asked to translate ideas, information or processes into diagrams, graphs/charts, models, drawings, photos or displays. Readings and investigations could culminate in an audio-visual product, such as a slide-tape, videotape or computer program. Criteria for expressive products need to be pre-determined (although a margin for originality and insight should perhaps be allowed).

For exceptionally good products (both print and non-print) teachers could request permission from the student to make a copy to use as an example or for demonstration materials in future courses. (Such a request is a great compliment to the student.)

S. Jorgensen. (1987). *Instructional Resource Booklet for the Graduate Teaching Assistants.* The Center for Instructional Services. Old Dominion University.

TESTING AND GRADING

Lecturing and other classroom activities are often seen as the fun part of teaching, while evaluating student work and assigning grades is less appealing. Unfortunately, for many students the grade is at least as important as class content.

ASKING THE RIGHT QUESTIONS

The first problem in testing is choosing the right things to test. Fortunately, selecting a concise set of learning objectives for the students makes test questions follow naturally. We are all familiar with such cases as the one in which the instructor states that the course objective is to "understand the broad sweep of history, the influences of social and economic factors on the course of events, and the way history relates things globally." The instructor then follows this with a 100-item multiple-choice exam, asking for names, dates, and places! This may sound ludicrous, but similar divergences occur between the first day of many classes and the first exams.

Tests are diagnostic tools, helping students identify areas they understand and those they do not. Tests can motivate since almost all students work harder to do well on exams. Studying for tests causes students to consider, evaluate, organize, synthesize, or apply material as they prepare. Finally, tests reward students who have achieved well.

The first step in test construction is to list course goals. Not all of these are easily measured, but this does not waive our responsibility to list such goals and at least attempt to develop relative test questions. Devising test items to examine students' synthesizing or evaluating abilities is difficult, but this does not justify asking only questions that test memorization of facts.

Recognize the purposes of testing. In a lecture we may use deductive reasoning to lead students to faulty conclusions, then back up to help them know where their reasoning failed. That can be instructive. The same exercise, however, on an exam that will figure into a student's grade does not have the same educational merit. We really are not out to trick students on exams, for that does not indicate anything meaningful about how much a student knows. Use clear statements, as unambiguously worded as possible. If you want to discriminate between shades of meaning, make it clear what point you are addressing.

If our goal is to encourage students to learn and to reward them for doing it well, psychology indicates that we should encourage and reward them frequently. Frequent testing has another advantage. When a student has a bad day or when we construct an exam that does not measure accurately, it is easy to spot and to handle separately if there are several test scores. If there are only one or two grades, it is far more difficult to define the true level of student accomplishment.

To enhance the self-assessment and motivating values of exams, they should be returned promptly. It is also useful to go over returned tests, helping students see what misunderstanding on their part caused errors. This may also reveal some problems with the exam.

Ohmer Milton, former Director of the Learning Research Center and Professor Emeritus, UTK, reports that the two most frequently asked questions on college campuses are "Will that be on

Humphreys, L. and Wickersham, B. (1986). *A handbook of resources for new instructors at UTK.* Learning Research Center, University of Tennessee, Knoxville.

the test?" and "Will the test be essay or objective?" We can easily see the educational impact of an answer to the first question. For the second, studies have shown that students prepare differently for essay versus objective (true-false, multiple-choice) tests. Essay exams cause students to evaluate, synthesize, and organize. They are also the most difficult to grade. Short answer questions test information recall and analytic or problem-solving skills. Multiple choice exams are the most difficult to construct well, but done correctly, they test both information recall and concept application. True-false questions are the most difficult to phrase well and are more subject to flawed evaluation, since a student can guess with a 50 percent probability of success.

GRADING

Grades are used in ways much broader than they appear immediately in a classroom context. Giving a student a "D" or an "F" may be appropriate, and may prove a sobering learning experience. Grades are not just communications between the instructor and the student, however, for they affect retention at the university, admission to graduate schools, abilities to secure employment, relationships with family and friends, self-esteem, and a host of other extra-curricular concerns. Add to this the fact that we often pack grades with other information, such as a reward for classroom participation or a penalty for a late paper or missed classes. The situation is further confused by the fact that there is no universal standard for the meaning of a "C" (or any other letter). To some a "C" indicates marginal work, barely acceptable, while to others it shows adequate, acceptable performance, but no extra initiative projects completed. Finally, the whole scheme is assigned a greater precision than it actually has by computing grade point averages to the second decimal place. The result is a seriously flawed measure with awesome weight. We cannot solve immediately the problems surrounding grades themselves, but we can work to see that grades going into the system are as accurate and meaningful as possible.

The first step is to grade accurately. Make each test item as clear as you can. Ask a colleague to review the test before it is given to identify any unintended ambiguities or hidden meanings. Take the exam yourself before you begin grading and note the answers you expect. Decide how to allocate points for answers that give only some of the information you want. As you grade, be alert for a pattern of wrong answers that signals a second (valid but unintended) interpretation for a question. If an item misleads students so that most answers do not address the points you wanted, discard it.

After grading an exam, list the kinds and number of erroneous responses for each question. Use this list to identify questions that discriminate well. After a few years of honing, an instructor builds a bank of several hundred reliable and valid questions with which to construct literally thousands of different exams.

Throughout the quarter, use a variety of evaluation methods. Different test formats stress different kinds of learning. Outside projects, such as papers or problem sets, give a different dimension to evaluations. If an assignment is graded on several criteria (for example content and grammar in a term paper), assign and record these grades separately. It is easier to respond to a potential employer's request for information about an applicant's problem-solving or writing ability by looking at grades assigned on different pieces of work, than by considering only a final course grade.

Be open, honest, and fair with students. Discuss tests both before and after they are given. If a student questions a grade, reread the paper without reference to the grade originally assigned, and attempt to determine a grade as you would have initially. If you have made a mistake, admit it and change the grade. Also offer to do things to overcome any potential harm from the incorrect grade, such as writing a letter to parents or a coach, or contacting the Veteran's Affairs or an admissions counsellor's office. If your grade agrees with the first evaluation, share with the student the basis for your evaluation. Listen to the student's interpretation and point out any flaws in logic. Keep accurate records, and retain grade records for several years. Your department may require you to leave your grade records with the department, so make sure your grading scheme is clearly indicated.

Grades are very imperfect measures, and at times it is not clear what they are measuring. Do your part by being clear to yourself and to your students as to what a grade means.

MARKING

Grading can be one of the most interesting duties performed by a TA, but so often turns out to be the most tedious. The type and amount of marking done by a TA depends largely on the course lecturer, though it can be modified by the TA in a number of ways. The modifications can serve several purposes. They may shorten the marking time, make the marking more accurate and equal, and allow the TA some say in the determination of criteria for and objectives of the marking process. All are desirable and give the TA both confidence in his approach and a chance to rationalize any philosophical issues that may concern him.

There comes a time for every TA (and the earlier the better) when he must accept the possibility that he will have a major role in passing or failing a student. Think about this early and think clearly. The TA is very familiar with the inequalities that exist in any marking scheme. Very early in the term, ask the lecturer to clarify his position on marking. Analyze your own outlook and preconceptions. Together, work out an approach to the philosophy of marking. Determine your criteria for the differences between grades; e.g. between a B+ and an A-. Talk to your peers on this issue and determine their approach. Don't just let this worry run around the back of your mind, but bring it out into the open, and be prepared to modify your approach on the basis of experience and information.

Once you have determined your approach, be prepared to modify it as necessary. The most annoying experience for a TA is having the prospect of 50 papers to mark, knowing that each one will take 20 minutes. The following are some hints on shortening the process. However, never should the quality of the marking be lowered to achieve this. If the time spent is consistently too long, discuss the problem with the course lecturer.

a.   Use a red pen so that your comments stand out.

b.   Mark by question, moving through the same question in each paper.

c.   Set up an ideal marking scheme beforehand, after reading several papers to determine the kinds of points you expect to be made to gain marks. For essays, determine in advance how much emphasis you are going to place on content, organization, style, and language.

d.   If there are other TAs on your course, share the setting up of the questions, the marking scheme and the process of marking. This procedure helps in solving the problem of differing approaches to marking the same question.

e.   Take regular breaks to ensure that you don't penalize students because you are tired or bored.

f.   After initial experience, modify the type and number of answers demanded such that you feel comfortable in accepting it.

Cotton, A. (1979). *Guidelines for teaching assistants in Geography.* Geography Department, Teaching Resource Office, University of Waterloo.

Now that you have a reasonable amount of work and an efficient approach, consider the following to achieve the finest quality results.

a. Mark clearly and positively so that the student knows which points were desirable. If parts of an answer were clearly wrong, say so, but suggest alternative approaches or answers, so that the student knows where he went wrong.

b. Don't be miserable, sarcastic or arrogant. This is far from the best way to approach a subject if you are trying to be positive. It leads to alienation.

c. Add up carefully and record marks clearly in a place where you won't lose them. It's often a good idea to record marks on two sheets to be safe. Avoid leaving papers lying on your desk. Keep them in a folder in a drawer so you can be sure who has handed them in and who hasn't.

d. Where desirable, comment on the paper as a whole and make suggestions for improvement. Let constructive criticism be your approach. Also comment on the parts of the paper or lab exercise that have been well done. A little praise may lead to a better effort next time.

e. If a mistake is common to many papers, save yourself some time by commenting on it to the class as a whole the next time you meet with them. In this way, each individual is more likely to learn from the mistake.

f. When dealing with essay questions, consider the points made in the answer, but mark the question as a whole.

g. On occasion, when work is being done as a learning exercise but is not being marked for student record purposes, the answers to questions can be marked by the group. Students can either correct and/or mark their own papers or each others'. In this way, the correcting and marking becomes part of the learning process.

h. Discussion of the best answers can be useful to the whole group of students. Take care not to embarrass the student whose answers you use by raising him on a pedestal in front of the class.

i. Collect due papers in such a way that there is no doubt as to whether the student has or has not handed the paper in. Hand back papers during the class to each student individually. Do not leave them outside your office for just anyone to take.

TESTING

Constructing tests is a serious concern of most instructors, and an important part of most courses. Formative testing can help instructors and students keep track of the kind and amount of learning that is taking place. Summative testing can provide important information about how much has been learned by the end of a unit, or by mid-semester, or by the end of the term.

The following list of items was derived from several different student evaluation forms from several different institutions. If you can answer "yes" to all items you are an outstanding constructor of tests.

1. Tests are fair and objective.

2. Students have an opportunity to discuss tests at a later date.

3. Tests are effectively integrated with the course.

4. Expectations concerning performance standards are clearly specified at the start of the course.

5. Tests avoid stressing unnecessary memorization.

6. Test items are not unreasonably detailed.

7. Tests are returned promptly.

8. Tests are of appropriate length.

A. OBJECTIVE TESTS

Listed below you will find a number of helpful hints if you need to construct multiple-choice tests.

First, group the test items by type. Second, increase item difficulty from the beginning to the end of the test. Third, increase the taxonomy level (from knowledge to comprehension to application to analysis to synthesis to evaluation). Fourth, the order of items should parallel the order of instruction as much as possible.

Other tips for generating multiple-choice tests follow.

1. The problem should be stated clearly in the stem (the stem is that part of the test item that precedes the choices).

2. Put most of the wording in the stem, making the wording of the choices as brief as possible.

3. The stem should be stated in positive terms whenever possible.

4. Grammar should be consistent (tenses, etc.)

S. Rollins. (1987). *Tips on Teaching.* Instructional Development Center, Bryant College.

5. Avoid verbal cues (e.g., same word in stem and answer.)

6. The distractors (incorrect items) should be plausible.

7. Correct answers should be placed in random positions.

8. Overlapping alternatives should be avoided.

9. Avoid textbook language.

10. Provide the same number of possible choices for each test item.

B. ESSAY TESTS

As with objective test items, those items that are developed for essay tests must be constructed with care. Essay test items tend to be of two main types, "restricted" response or "extended" response. Restricted response limits the answer and the kind of response that is expected is carefully defined. For example, "list" or "define" or "give reasons." Such items serve best when the instructor's goal is to elicit a demonstration of comprehension, analysis, and application; they are not as good for integration, organization, or the development of new responses. Extended response permits much more freedom for students to determine the form and scope of their responses. They tend to be more open-ended kinds of items that allow students to demonstrate synthesis, evaluation skills, creative integration of ideas, overall evaluation of materials and concepts, and problem solving. One drawback is that such responses are more difficult to evaluate.

Some suggestions for the construction of essay tests are:

1. use essay questions for complex learning outcomes only;

2. relate the questions as directly as possible to the learning outcomes you want to measure;

3. formulate questions that present a clear task to the student;

4. do not permit students a choice of questions unless the learning outcome requires it;

5. provide ample time for answering and suggest a time limit for each answer.

Because essay tests are more difficult to score than objective type tests, it is important to determine rules for scoring before the test is distributed. Some suggested rules for scoring essay tests follow.

1. Evaluate answers to essay questions in terms of the learning outcomes being measured.

2. Score restricted response answers by a point method, using a model answer as a guide.

3. Score extended response answers by a rating method, using defined criteria as a guide.

4. Evaluate all of the student's answers to one question before proceeding to the next question.

5. Evaluate answers to essay questions without knowing the identity of the writer.

6. When possible, have two or more persons grade each answer.

TESTING THE TEST

Based on research identifying good practices associated with the construction of multiple-choice test questions, John C. Ory of the Measurement and Research Division of the Office of Instructional Resources at the University of Illinois offers the following checklist for evaluating your multiple-choice tests. Take one of your multiple-choice exams, consider the questions in it, and proceed through the checklist.

When possible, the author:

_____ stated the item as a direct question rather than as an incomplete statement.

_____ presented a definite, explicit, and singular question or problem in the stem.

_____ eliminated excessive verbiage or irrelevant information from the stem.

_____ included in the stem any word(s) that might have otherwise been repeated in each alternative.

_____ used negatively stated stems sparingly. When used, underlined and/or capitalized the negative word(s).

_____ made all alternative plausible and attractive to the less-knowledgeable or skillful student.

_____ made the alternatives grammatically parallel with each other, and consistent with the stem.

_____ made the alternatives mutually exclusive.

_____ when possible, presented alternatives in some logical order (e.g., chronologically; most to least).

_____ made sure there was only one correct or best response per item.

_____ made alternatives approximately equal in length.

John C. Ory, *The Teaching Professor*, 1 (9). Magna Publications, Inc., 2718 Dryden Drive, Madison, WI. Annual subscription $39.

_____ avoided irrelevant clues such as grammatical structure, well-known verbal associations, or connections between stem and answer.

_____ used at least four alternatives for each item.

_____ randomly distributed the correct response among the alternative positions throughout the test, having approximately the same proportion of alternatives a, b, c, d and e as the correct response.

_____ used the alternatives "none of the above" and "all of the above" sparingly. When used, such alternatives were occasionally the correct answer.

Summary

Some of the points contained in this section are:

- Regular assignments and clear expectations help keep students up-to-date in class. (p. 118)

- Correct and hand back assignments promptly. (p. 118)

- Grade one problem at a time, shuffling the papers in between. (p. 119)

- Inform the class of averages on exams and quizzes. (p. 120)

- Hand out solution sheets after tests have been graded and handed back. (p. 120)

- Pretest the exams to check length, difficulty, and wording of questions. (p. 121)

- Think in terms of diverse writing assignments and a broad range of inquiry and expressive assignments to evaluate students. (p. 122)

- Test questions follow naturally from well-selected learning objectives. (p. 123)

- Be alert for patterns of incorrect responses. (p. 124)

- Keep a list of good questions for future use. (p. 124)

- Use a variety of evaluation methods; exams, problem sets, papers, projects. (p. 124)

- Keep accurate records and retain them for several years. (p. 125)

- With the lecturer, work out an approach/philosophy to grading. (p. 126)

- Use a red pen to mark clearly and positively; don't be sarcastic. (p. 126)

- Set up an ideal marking scheme beforehand. (p. 126)

- Take regular breaks. (p. 126)

- Add points and record grades carefully; keep them in a safe place. (p. 127)

- Comment on the paper as a whole and make suggestions for improvements. (p. 127)

- Mark essay questions as a whole, while considering the points that were made. (p. 127)

- Sometimes answers can be marked as a group. (p. 127)

- A discussion of the best answers can be helpful to the whole group, but don't embarrass students. (p. 127)

- Collect due papers so there is no question of who handed papers in. (p. 127)

- Compare your multiple choice test with the checklist provided. (p. 130)

SPECIAL TOPICS
The Rest of the Book

Part II

12
Cheating and Plagiarism

One brisk autumn day, our three heroes decide to go to a football game with a couple of undergraduate friends, Franklin and Jeff. Mercedes has never seen a game before, and Steve offers to explain it to her. At halftime, the conversation turns (of course) to teaching.

"Explain the part about putting the sack over the quarterback again."

"You mean sacking the quarterback? Sure—"

"Forget about that," Maureen says, "I want to know what you're going to do about those two projects you got handed in that were almost identical."

"I'm not sure," sighs Mercedes. "I only got them Friday, so I haven't had a chance to look them over really well yet. They were pretty similar, though."

"Do you think somebody cheated?" asks Jeff.

"I'd hate to accuse anybody of that, but it's very hard to write two computer programs independently and have them come out that close. If I think they're plagiarized, I'll talk to my supervisor before I do anything."

"Good idea," says Maureen. "My first year, I accused a student of plagiarism without really checking it out or talking with anyone first, and I got into a lot of trouble. Make real sure you know what you're doing before you confront anyone. It'll save you a lot of grief."

"I've got to proctor an exam next week. Do people cheat on exams these days?" Steve asks.

"Come on, it's the '80s. Everybody does it," Franklin shoots back. "Life is very competitive these days, and some people will use any edge they can get."

Maureen, a little taken aback, says, "I don't know if it's as bad as all that, but there are people who'll try to sneak a peek here and there. How many people are you proctoring?"

"Forty or so."

"Ouch. Be careful. Watch for roving eyes and such. You've just got to be real observant and on top of things to make sure that nothing funny goes on."

"Hey, I didn't mean to say that *everybody* cheats on exams, but I've seen it happen a lot, that's all," says Franklin, a little sheepishly. "I hope everything goes OK for you guys next week."

"Me, too," says Mercedes. "I also hope that we do better in this game in the second half. You suppose we can catch up?"

"Sure," says Steve. "it's only 35 points. Comebacks like that happen all the time."

CHEATING

The University takes the position that the best way to handle cheating is first to attempt to prevent it and second, if it occurs, to deal with it swiftly and decisively.

Plagiarism is the most prevalent form of cheating on campus, and it is also the hardest to prevent. Plagiarism in a term paper or other written assignment cannot be proven unless the original source is found. An instructor who suspects that a student has plagiarized a source should compare the questionable material with other samples of the student's writing, if possible. An instructor should always feel free to contact any student he or she suspects of plagiarism and inquire about the student's use of sources and methodology. Some students cannot distinguish between paraphrasing and plagiarism, and many do not understand the implications of cheating and plagiarism. Teachers can refer students who need to improve their writing skills to the facilities on campus which specialize in such assistance.

PREVENTING CHEATING

There are several methods of dealing with cheating, both during the taking of an examination and on the basis of already completed examinations and term papers. The best of these is to devise examinations that provide fewer opportunities for cooperative student efforts and eliminate the possibility of cheating. Open book exams are an especially effective anti-cheating device. It is essential that someone be present to proctor all examinations. Proctors are advised simply to watch the class carefully in order to discourage the most common forms of cheating during a test: wandering eyes and talking. Both are extremely difficult to prove and to prosecute without at least two additional witnesses to the incident. The best solution to the problem of wandering eyes is to require the students suspected of cheating to change their seats, and the rest of the class should be aware of the move; this creates a chilling effect that should deter other students from attempting to copy their neighbor's paper. Proctoring of examinations should be most strict at the point when many of the students are completing and handing in their work at once, and there are opportunities for talking and even exchanging answers or papers.

Objective examinations, especially those which are machine-scored, are the easiest to cheat on of all exams. The essay examination appears to be the least conducive to cheating of all test forms. However, the practice of distributing several essay questions to a class before an examination with the understanding that one or more of those questions will appear on the test facilitates cheating. Students may turn in prepared answers to the questions. Teachers may prevent this type of cheating by examining blue books prior to the exam, or requiring students to begin writing their essays on odd pages.

Morrow, R. (1976). *What every TA should know.* In *The TA at UCLA: A handbook for teaching assistants. (1977-78).* The Regents of the University of California.

CHEATING, LYING, AND OTHER NASTY THINGS

There are formal ways of dealing with cheating in exams. These methods are well established and the chances of you having to deal to any extent with this are minimal. In the laboratory or seminar situation, however, a number of devious things can take place. Students may copy the work of other students and hand it in as their own. This may happen with the knowledge of the student whose work was copied, or his work may be stolen. The theft sometimes takes place off the TA's desk. Make sure that the students hand in their work directly to you. Put it away safely in a drawer.

Plagiarism may also take place, though it is often difficult to detect. In all cases, except that of theft, a quiet chat with the students concerned on the values of being honest and the penalties for being caught cheating, suffices to clear up the problem. In the case of theft it is best to decide on a course of action in consultation with the professor or lecturer. In many cases, students do not realize what constitutes plagiarism and it would be beneficial to discuss the subject with them during one of the early teaching sessions.

Cotton, A. (1979). *Guidelines for teaching assistants in Geography*. Geography Department, Teaching Resource Office, University of Waterloo.

PREVENTING STUDENT ACADEMIC DISHONESTY

The best ways to prevent academic dishonesty are to inform students of standards for scholarship and conduct and minimize the opportunities for cheating or plagiarism. The following ideas, designed to encourage academic honesty, are based on the teaching practices of Berkeley faculty and graduate student instructors, as well as ideas from other universities. You may wish to consider implementing one or more of these tips.

GENERAL STRATEGIES

Spend 10-15 minutes discussing standards of academic scholarship and conduct. Describe acceptable and unacceptable behavior, giving examples of plagiarism, impermissible collaboration, and other practices relevant to your class. Explain that cheating will not be tolerated and discuss University policies, procedures, and penalties for academic violations. Some departments hand out written materials that define cheating and plagiarism and require students to sign a statement that they have read and understood the material.

Make sure students know the criteria for evaluating their performance. Review their work throughout the term so that they know *you* know their abilities and achievement levels.

Develop a climate and group norms that support honesty. For example, you may wish to take a vote in class to conduct the exams under the honor system (without proctors).

Learn to recognize signs of stress in students. Make students aware of campus resources that they can turn to for help if their grades are low or if they feel under pressure.

Ensure equal access to study materials. Establish a file in the library or departmental office of old homework assignments, exams, and papers.

Make students feel as though they can succeed in your class without having to resort to dishonesty. Encourage students to come talk with you if they are having difficulties.

If you suspect students of cheating or plagiarizing material, confront them directly. Talk with them about it. Do not conclude that cheating has taken place without hearing the student's side.

PLAGIARISM

Clarify the distinctions between plagiarism, paraphrasing, and direct citation. Provide students with instances of correct and incorrect ways to use others' ideas and words. You might want to share the following example with your class (from *The Random House Handbook* by Frederick Crews, New York: Random House, 1984, pp. 405-406):

Davis, B. Gross. (1987). *Preventing Student Academic Dishonesty.* Office of Educational Development, University of California, Berkeley.

Consider the following source and three ways that a student might be tempted to make use of it:

Source:
The joker in the European pack was Italy. For a time hopes were entertained of her as a force against Germany, but these disappeared under Mussolini. In 1935 Italy made a belated attempt to participate in the scramble for Africa by invading Ethiopia. It was clearly a breach of the covenant of the League of Nations for one of its members to attack another. France and Great Britain, as great powers, Mediterranean powers, and African colonial powers, were bound to take the lead against Italy at the league. But they did so feebly and half-heartedly because they did not want to alienate a possible ally against Germany. The result was the worst possible: the league failed to check aggression, Ethiopia lost her independence, and Italy was alienated after all.[1]

[1] J.M. Roberts, *History of the World* (New York: Knopf, 1976), p. 845.

Version A:
Italy, one might say, was the joker in the European deck. When she invaded Ethiopia, it was clearly a breach of the covenant of the League of Nations; yet the efforts of England and France to take the lead against her were feeble and half-hearted. It appears that those great powers had no wish to alienate a possible ally against Hitler's rearmed Germany.

Comment: Clearly plagiarism. Though the facts cited are public knowledge, the stolen phrases aren't. Note that the writer's interweaving of his own words with the source's do not render him innocent of plagiarism.

Version B:
Italy was the joker in the European deck. Under Mussolini in 1935, she made a belated attempt to participate in the scramble for Africa by invading Ethiopia. As J. M. Roberts points out, this violated the covenant of the League of Nations.[1] But France and Britain, not wanting to alienate a possible ally against Germany, put up only feeble and half-hearted opposition to the Ethiopian adventure. The outcome, as Roberts observes, was "the worst possible: the league failed to check aggression, Ethiopia lost her independence, and Italy was alienated after all."[2]

[1] J.M. Roberts, *History of the World* (New York: Knopf, 1976), p. 845.
[2] Roberts, p. 845.

Comment: Still plagiarism. The two correct citations of Roberts serve as a kind of alibi for the appropriating of other, unacknowledged phrases. But the alibi has no force: some of Roberts' words are again being presented as the writer's.

Version C:
Much has been written about German rearmament and militarism in the period 1933-1939. But Germany's dominance in Europe was by no means a foregone conclusion. The fact is that the balance of power might have been tipped against Hitler if one or two things had turned out differently. Take Italy's gravitation toward an alliance with Germany, for example. That alliance seemed so very far from inevitable that Britain and France actually muted their criticism of the Ethiopian invasion in the hope of remaining friends with Italy. They opposed the Italians in the League of Nations, as J.M. Roberts observes, "feebly and half-heartedly because they did not want to alienate a possible ally against Germany."[1] Suppose Italy, France, and Britain had retained a certain common interest. Would Hitler have been able to get away with his remarkable bluffing and bullying in the later thirties?

[1] J.M. Roberts, *History of the World* (New York: Knopf, 1976), p. 845.

Comment: No plagiarism. The writer has been influenced by the public facts mentioned by Roberts, but he hasn't tried to pass off Roberts' conclusions as his own. The one clear borrowing is properly acknowledged.

PAPER TOPICS

Assign specific topics. Design topics that are likely to require new research, that stress "thinking about it" more than "looking it up," and that are challenging but not overwhelming. Topics that are too difficult invite cheating, as do boring, trivial, and uninteresting topics.

Limit students' choices of broad paper topics. If given complete freedom, students may flounder and turn to commercially produced term papers or "file" papers as an easy out.

Change the topics or assignments as often as possible. This prevents students from simply appropriating an essay from someone who has already taken your course.

DEMYSTIFYING WRITING

Give a short lecture on how to research and write a paper or essay. With this information, students will feel more confident that they know what is expected of them.

Discuss openly in class the difficulties of writing. Help students understand that the anxieties or blocks they face are a normal part of the writing process. "If, in the classroom, you emphasize the stages of the composing process and the normal tribulations of every writer, your students may be less likely to conclude that cheating is the only feasible way of getting from an assigned topic to a finished paper" (English 1A-1B *Handbook for TAs*, p. 18).

During the term schedule a variety of short in-class papers. In-class assignments help students develop their writing skills and help you determine their abilities. Instructors who assign only one paper a term have a hard time judging whether that assignment is the student's own work.

Early in the course require students to come in to discuss their research or essay topics. Again, later in the course, ask them to share outlines and to discuss how they plan to organize and present their ideas and findings. This approach not only helps students write better papers, but also allows the instructor to see students' ideas develop.

PREPARING AND SUBMITTING PAPERS

Require students to submit first drafts. Giving students feedback on their first drafts can help them improve their writing skills.

Request that final versions of papers be handed in with drafts. Ask for note cards and outlines as well.

Specify the format for papers. Instructions for the styling of the headings, footnotes, margins, and so on for essays or manuscripts discourage students from purchasing or using others' papers.

Accept only originals. Or ask students to turn in the original and one duplicate. Keep the copies for your files to consult the next time you teach to identify pirated or purloined papers.

Collect papers from students during class. If papers are turned in at a department or faculty office, consider using locked mailboxes with slots for collection.

Require students to return their papers after they have reviewed your comments. Keep the papers for a year and then let students know they may collect them if they wish.

EXAM QUESTIONS

Change exam questions as often as is practical. Ask graduate student instructors and students to submit prospective questions. With judicious editing, some will be appropriate for the exam and others could form the basis of an item pool.

For multiple-choice exams, use alternate forms. Scramble the order of questions, and color code the different exams.

Keep exams, grade books, and rosters safe. Store them in locked cabinets, desks or file drawers in your office.

TEST ADMINISTRATION FOR LARGE EXAMINATION SESSIONS

Make certain that a faculty member or graduate student instructor is in the room at all times. During an exam arrange for proctoring, unless your class is run on an honor system.

Seat students in alternate chairs. Have students place personal belongings on the floor rather than in empty seats. If needed, schedule an additional room.

In large classes, consider seating students in preassigned groups. For example, students could sit by section so that graduate student instructors can determine if all their students are in attendance and that "ringers" are not taking tests. Or, check photo IDs displayed on desks against class lists to be certain that each student takes his or her own exam.

In rooms with seat numbers, keep a seating chart. Hand out bluebooks or exams with pre-recorded seat numbers.

Make certain that students have cleared the memories on their calculators. Before you distribute the exam or as students enter the room, check the calculators' memories.

Supply scratch paper. Do not permit students to use their own paper or pages of their bluebooks.

Station proctors throughout the room. Have them pay particular attention when students are turning in their completed exams.

Have proctors or graduate student instructors collect exams from students. Do not allow students to rush chaotically to turn their bluebooks in.

Require students to sign an attendance sheet when they turn in their exams. Count those present at the exam to make certain that the number of examinees matches the number of exams.

BLUEBOOKS

Require students to write only on the left-handed pages. Or ask students to leave a certain number of pages blank at the beginning of their bluebooks.

GRADING

Clearly mark incorrect answers or blank spaces. Use an inked "X" or slash mark.

If you permit regrading of exams, take precautions. Throughout the term photocopy those exams or quizzes of students who initially ask for regrading. Or photocopy a sample of all exams before returning them to students.

Return exams and assignments to students in person. Do not leave them in the department office or on your desk for students to pick up.

Consider switching to an absolute or criterion-referenced system of grading rather than grading on the curve.

Summary

Some of the points contained in this section are:

- "Plagiarism in a term paper or other written assignment cannot be proven unless the original source is found." (p. 136)

- "Some students cannot distinguish between paraphrasing and plagiarism and do not understand the implications of cheating and plagiarism." Explain these concepts thoroughly early in the semester. (pp. 136, 138)

- "Open book exams are an especially effective anti-cheating device." (p. 136)

- Proctors should be available at all exams to watch for roving eyes and talking, and should be especially alert when many students are handing in their papers. (p. 136)

- Change the seats of students who are acting suspiciously during an exam. (p. 136)

- Objective exams are the easiest to cheat on; essay exams make it more difficult to do so. (p. 136)

- Ask students to begin writing essay answers on odd pages to prevent the use of previously prepared answers. (pp. 136, 142)

- Keep students' papers in a safe place to prevent them from being stolen and copied. (p. 137)

- A private, quiet chat about honesty should be sufficient to clear up a problem, except in cases of theft when you should consult with your supervisor. (p. 137)

- If you do encounter a case of plagiarism, talk with another knowledgeable person and consult with the department chair, your advisor, or the senior lecturer. (p. 137)

- Develop a climate and group norms that support honesty. (p.138)

- Make students feel as though they can succeed in your class without having to resort to dishonesty. (p.138)

- Change the topics or assignments as often as possible. (p. 140)

- During the term schedule a variety of short in-class papers. (p.140)

- Request that final versions of papers be handed in with their drafts. (p.141)

- In large group exams consider seating students in pre-assigned groups. (p. 141)

- Photocopy exams/quizzes of students who often ask for re-grading. (p. 142)

• We found the piece below particularly well written. Since it sums everything up so nicely, we opted to include it here rather than in the main section. It was taken, with permission, from *A Handbook of Resources for New Instructors at UTK*, Learning Resource Center, University of Tennessee, Knoxville, p. 12.

If you have ample reason to suspect a student of cheating or plagiarism, it is advisable first to share the evidence with your department head or director before acting. Be as positive as you can of guilt before questioning the student(s), since academic misconduct sometimes makes them liable for serious punishment. According to the seriousness of the offense, punishment can run the gamut from exoneration to exclusion from the University. Even the suggestion of guilt is upsetting to students, particularly if they are innocent.

13
Writing Letters of Recommendation

Maureen is reading through her mail one afternoon in her apartment when the phone rings. It's Steve.

"Hi, Steve. How's it going?"

"Oh, not bad. What's up tonight? Are you going to Rosemary's Place?"

"Yeah, probably. Oh, damn."

"What's the matter?"

"Oh, it's an old student of mine, asking me to write him a letter of recommendation. I never liked him, he wasn't too bright, and he only barely got a C from me. I can't write one of those 'Jim is an outstanding student who I know will go far' type letters."

"Then don't. Either don't write the letter, or tell the truth. In either case, you ought to let him know your feelings about doing it. He might not want you to after you tell him."

"That's tough to do. How do you tell someone you don't want to write a letter of recommendation for them?"

"How about, 'I don't want to write a letter of recommendation for you.'? Nice, simple, to the point. Look, you don't *have* to write these letters. You're doing him a favor. And he has the right to know what you think of him if it's not completely positive. I had a friend at my undergrad school who got nailed by a professor in a recommendation for graduate school. He almost didn't get in because the woman wrote an awful letter."

"Hmmm. I guess you're right. How did you get so smart?"

"Hanging around with you guys. That's in addition, of course, to my natural brilliance and charm."

"Bye, Steve. See you later."

145

LETTER OF RECOMMENDATION

Students may ask you to recommend them for a particular job, acceptance to another institution, or graduate school. If you do not feel you know the student well enough, simply explain why not. If you are willing to write the letter, do so promptly, while you still have the student and his or her performance sharply in mind. A carefully written and thoughtful letter takes time and you are a busy person, but remember that others have done and will do this same kind of chore for you.

Ask if there is a specific form to be used or whether a letter is needed. Have the student note the nature of the job or situation for which s/he is applying and any particular abilities that you might mention. Then be as specific as possible. Focus on the student's best points, but don't exaggerate; be honest. Be sure to define the context within which you knew the person, e.g., in class, as an advisor formally or informally, and state over what period of time. If you later see the student for whom you wrote the recommendation, ask about the results. This not only lets the student know you are interested but gives you feedback on your own letter-writing efforts.

Keep your old grade books for some time. Students may call upon you long after a class is finished. Some instructors make a habit of noting both good and not-so-good points about students in the margins of their grade books. This serves as a mental refresher if there has been some distance in thought or time since you last dealt with the student.

Keep in mind that you are legally responsible for statements you make in your recommendation, to the extent, at least, that you are liable for any deleterious remarks you make. If you have reason to be concerned about something you want to express, preface what you have to say with something like "To the best of my knowledge . . ." Remember that "libel and slander are both methods of defamation, the former being expressed by print, writing, pictures, or signs; the latter by oral expressions."[1]

Under the Educational Rights and Privacy Act, a student has the right to see a copy of your recommendation unless s/he is willing to sign a waiver. If you have no objections, this problem can be circumvented by giving a copy of the recommendation to the student.

Humphreys, L. and Wickersham, B. (1986). *A handbook of resources for new instructors at UTK.* Learning Research Center, University of Tennessee, Knoxville.
[1]Ajouelo v Auto-Soler Co. 61, Ga. App., 216.

LETTERS OF RECOMMENDATION

As a teacher, you will be an important influence on the lives of many students, and you may occasionally be called upon to write letters of recommendation to accompany a student's application for a summer job, full-time employment, or graduate school. If you remember the student's performance as commendable, you should have no difficulty with such a request.

However, if it has been some time since you taught the student or if you have any reservations regarding the level of performance, it is generally better to be straightforward about your position. The following suggestions may be helpful if you find yourself in such a situation.

RETAINING RECORDS

Save your class records! Although you may get to know your students quite well during a course, your recollection of individual students may become vague several months later. If your records and recall are not sufficient, you will need to set up an appointment to meet with the student. It may be advisable to ask the student to bring a brief resume to give you some insight into her/his goals and subsequent academic activities and achievements.

If you have some reservations about a student's performance, discuss them with the student. If the student appreciates your point of view, you can still write a positive letter of recommendation by citing the student's strong points as well as weaknesses. After all, most employers realize that there are few "perfect performers;" consequently, an honest appraisal may actually carry more weight than a gushing letter of unbridled praise. If you decide not to provide a letter of reference, however, be sure to let the student know.

THE LETTER OF RECOMMENDATION

When recommending a student, a standard business letter format on your department's letterhead is generally appropriate, unless other forms are provided. Specific formats and guidelines for letters of recommendation are sometimes specified by placement agencies and academic admissions offices, so be sure to consult the student about this detail. Be sure to get the full name, title, and address of the person to whom the reference should be addressed; and be sure to get the student's full name with correct spelling. Mistakes in this area can understandably have a negative effect on the reviewer of letters of recommendation.

A one-page letter is usually sufficient to provide the typical information, including the following: your relationship to the student; how long you have known her or him; your comments about the person's skills, performance in your class, and present position or responsibilities; observations regarding the individual's strengths, weaknesses, initiative and motivation; and your recommendation regarding how the above information will qualify the student for the job or course of study under consideration. Also include your title, telephone number, and address in case the employer should wish to contact you for further information, and keep a copy of the letter for your files.

Handbook for Graduate Teaching Assistants. Office of Instructional Development, the Graduate School, University of Georgia, 1987.

Finally, ask the student to let you know the outcome. Writing letters of recommendation is a time consuming chore, and it can be very rewarding to know that you had an opportunity to help to advance a worthy student in the same way that the recommendations of your former teachers helped you.

WRITING LETTERS OF RECOMMENDATION

Students may ask you to write letters of recommendation for them for jobs, graduate schools, or transfers to other undergraduate institutions. Find out what the student is applying for; this will guide you in what qualities to stress in the letter. In general, include the following information:

1. Describe your relationship to the student. State how long you have known him and in what capacity.

2. Discuss the student's intellectual ability by comparing him to other students with whom you have worked.

3. Describe the student's attitude toward academic work. Were assignments completed promptly, carefully, and with enthusiasm?

4. If it is applicable to the situation, describe the student's performance in a laboratory situation. Comment on his preparation for labs and understanding of the experiments' underlying principles. You may also wish to note whether or not you would trust the student to work in a laboratory without supervision.

5. The student's communication skills, both verbal and written, should also be described. Are the skills appropriate to the work being contemplated?

6. Finally, discuss any personal characteristics of the student which you believe are relevant.

If possible, use specific examples or anecdotes to illustrate the points you make in your letter. Focus on what it is that makes this student different from others, but be careful not to overdue your praise. Be honest above all else. If you are approached for a recommendation and you feel that you cannot, in good conscience, write a positive letter of recommendation, suggest that the student ask someone else.

Your letter should be typed on your department's official stationery. If the student was in a lab or recitation section of which you were in charge, you may want to ask the instructor for the class to co-sign the letter of recommendation with you.

Robert A. Wolke (Ed.) (1984). *A handbook for teaching assistants.* (2nd edition). Office of Faculty Development, University of Pittsburgh.

Summary

Some of the points contained in this section are:

- If you don't know the student well enough, or if the student did not do well in your course, explain why you can't write the letter. (pp. 146, 147)

- Write letters carefully and promptly. (p. 146)

- Ask if a specific form is to be used. (p. 146)

- Ask student for any specific abilities that should be noted. (p. 146)

- Focus on the student's good points but don't exaggerate. (p. 146)

- Define the context in which you know the student. (p. 146)

- Keep your old grade books for reference. (p. 146)

- Keep in mind that you are legally responsible for the remarks that you make. (p. 146)

- If you're concerned about what you want to say, use the phrase "to the best of my knowledge." (p. 146)

- Request a resume from or set up an appointment with the student to refresh your memory. (p.147)

- Be sure to use the student's full name and spell it correctly. (p.147)

- Describe the student's strengths, weaknesses, initiative and motivation. (p. 147)

- Discuss the student's intellectual ability by comparing him/her to other students with whom you have worked. (p. 149)

- Describe the student's attitude toward academic work. (p. 149)

- Describe the appropriateness of the student's communication skills to the work being contemplated. (p.149)

- Use specific examples or anecdotes to illustrate the points you make in your letter. (p.149)

- Type the letter on your department's official stationery. (p.149)

14

Relationship with Students

Maureen sits in her office one afternoon, reading. A student in her Freshman Composition class, Rich, timidly approaches the door and knocks lightly. "Excuse me, Miss O'Reilly?"

"Hmmm? Oh, hi, Richard. Come on in and have a seat. And you can call me Maureen. I prefer it, actually."

"Oh, uh, thanks. Have you got a few minutes?"

"Sure. What can I do for you?"

"Well, I like the way you're teaching the class. You do it very well, but I've got a few questions about the reading for next class. Could you help me?"

"Of course. What do you want to know?"

They spend ten minutes or so discussing the merits of Faulkner versus Steinbeck. Then, Maureen says, "I think you've got the gist of what I was trying to get across. You feel better about it now?"

"Yeah, a lot better. Ummm . . ."

"Anything else?"

"Well, I was just wondering if, uh, if you were, um, busy tonight and maybe we could get a pizza or something," Rich says, looking down at the floor.

Maureen takes a deep breath. "I don't think that's a good idea right now, Richard. When you teach, you have to be very careful not to get too involved with people in your classes—it looks bad, and it can lead to real trouble if it goes too far. I like you a lot; I think you're very bright, and your work so far has been good. Keep it up. Maybe we could have a cup of coffee over at the union sometime and talk. How does that sound?"

"Oh, sure, I just thought . . ."

"Don't worry about it. Maybe early next week? I'm a little swamped right now and *you* have a paper due on Monday, don't you?"

"Yep. I'm going to go to the library and work on it right now. I'll see you later. Bye."

"Take care. See you soon."

HOW FORMAL?

Most professors, while leaving the matter ultimately up to the individual, prefer TAs to maintain a certain distance between themselves and their students. Some TAs choose to remain on a second-name basis with their students, and conduct their classes with some semblance of formality; your decision regarding this depends partly on your personality, but as one TA put it: "I'm giving them a grade, so how can I be their friend?"

A few TAs socialize with their students outside of class, but this may cause difficulties when you come to mark the paper of the student with whom you were wassailing and carousing the night before. Many TAs treat their students to a celebratory beer at the end of term, which brings us to the TA who took her students to the Campus Centre Pub, graciously accepted the twenty ryes her twenty class members insisted on buying for her, and ended up cruising up and down King Street in one of her student's cars along with eight other inebriates. They narrowly avoided being arrested.

Because the classes tend to be rather small, and you are unlikely to be much older than your students—although one twenty four old TA was asked by a student how well he remembered the Depression—the atmosphere is usually easy-going, relaxed and fairly informal. It is wise, however, to be careful of the language you use in class. By all means be conversational and colloquial in your speech, but while some of your students may be absolutely thrilled by your unscholarly damning, cursing, slanging and all-round unparliamentary scurrility, others may be offended. You could also have difficulties justifying your marginal "too colloquial" comment when the odd expletive starts turning up in their essays. Make it clear that you expect a certain formality in their written work.

You can easily alienate your class, not only by using offensive language, but by asking personal questions. There is the sorry tale of a TA who, when dealing with the subject of connotative language, took in photocopies of John Donne's poem, "The Comparison." Donne's popular claim to fame is hardly due to bashfulness in matters sexual, and this poem is, of course, no exception. The analysis of the poem was going very well until the TA reached the lines:

> Is not your last act harsh, and violent,
> As when a Plough a stony ground doth rent?

It must be said in defence of this TA, that it was very early in the morning and she had been up most of the night—marking papers, she maintains. Anyway, a resounding silence met her request for an interpretation of these lines so, recalling all that she had been told about drawing the students out, she asked all those who had ever had an orgasm to kindly raise their hands and offer some enlightenment as to how it might resemble a plough rattling over a rutty field. This was a mistake. True, one amiable Engineering student volunteered to come to the front of the room and give a demonstration, but the rest of the class broke up in embarrassed titters and was rendered incapable of further concentration for the rest of the morning.

Woodhead, J. (1979). *A manual for teaching assistants in the department of English.* Teaching Resource Office, University of Waterloo.

"TENDER IS THE TEACHER":
GETTING EMOTIONALLY INVOLVED

"Love is . . . my instructor sitting at her desk and looking out of the window while we are writing our assignments."

—from an English 109 essay, "Define an Abstraction by Means of Concrete Example."

"I couldn't help it. I can resist everything except temptation."

—Oscar Wilde, *Lady Windermere's Fan.*

You are, presumably, human, and therefore liable to fall in love. This is an unfortunate tendency, common to many humans, and students of English Literature seem particularly susceptible to it, probably because they spend so much time reading Lord Byron's love poetry and calling it Intellectual Curiosity. We cannot, therefore, ignore the possibility of your getting emotionally involved with one of your students.

Unfortunately, the scope of this manual cannot include a discussion of the nature of love, but it must be said that "falling in love" is, to a certain extent, an act of will; and, in theory at least, you can choose *not* to let it happen. If, however, you do find yourself knocked out, bowled over, swept off your feet, and other such metaphoric pleasantries, by one of your students, to the extent that you are rendered incapable of objectivity in marking his or her essays because every dangling modifier is like inscriptional music to your ears, you've got a problem. Take the problem to your professor. He or she will not be totally unsympathetic, and has probably had to deal with such matters before. The most obvious solution is to have the student transferred to another section.

This, of course, would be an extreme case. There are more likely to be times when you simply establish a special rapport with a particular student, or you may find yourself developing an aversion towards a student who quibbles with every grade you give him, throws chalk at you and indulges in other such antisocial behaviour. If, for whatever reason, you feel that you cannot be entirely objective in marking and grading a student's paper, you should at least take the paper to another TA for evaluation before giving the student "what he deserves."

It is easy enough to say that emotional involvement can be avoided by maintaining at least a minimum of "professional distance"; it is more difficult to put this strategy into practice, especially if one of your class members is not only very close in age to you, but highly intelligent, perceptive and communicative. If you find yourself faced with a passive and/or slow class, it is tempting to direct your teaching only at the one student who, in a sense, embodies your own effectiveness as a teacher because he seems to understand perfectly what you are trying to impart to the class, and is able to demonstrate that understanding in his written work. When you pose a question, it is tempting to continually pick out from the upstretched hands which are volunteering an answer, the student who will positively reinforce you by giving the correct answer every time. You should also bear in mind that the most vocal students

---

Woodhead, J. (1979). *A manual for teaching assistants in the department of English.* Teaching Resource Office, University of Waterloo.

are not necessarily the best at written work and you should not form "mental sets" based on bright-eyed enthusiasm in class.

Students are piqued by teachers who make a show of having their pets, especially if the student is known to receive high grades. They may show their resentment by lapsing into an increasingly silent hostility. They may begin to wonder—and so should you—"Is this student a favorite because he gets high grades, or does he get high grades because he is a favorite?"

Summary

Some of the points contained in this section are:

- How formal or informal you should be with your class depends on your personality. (p. 152)

- Be careful of the language you use in class. (p. 152)

- You can alienate your class by asking personal questions. (p. 152)

- If you are "swept off your feet" by a student, talk to your professor and possibly have the student transferred to another section. (p. 153)

- If you feel a special rapport or aversion for a particular student, ask another person to check on your grading of that student. (p. 153)

- Emotional involvement may be avoided by keeping a minimum professional distance; this is easier said than done. (p. 153)

- Avoid showing favoritism. (p. 154)

15
Problems with Students

Steve grunts as he slumps into a chair. Maureen and Mercedes are used to this by now.

"What's wrong, dear? Tough day at the office?" asks Maureen, with a broad smile on her face.

"Cute," says Steve, "real cute. Yes, in fact, I did have a tough day. Not only did my stat professor assign three chapters of readings and twenty problems for the weekend, but a guy in my recitation is giving me a hard time."

"Gee, that's too bad, Steve," says Mercedes. "What's the problem with your student?"

"Well, Phil's just a nuisance at times. He acts up in class, he almost never does the readings, and he's just generally obnoxious."

"Have you talked to him about it yet?"

"No . . . I wasn't sure how to handle it. I've just tried to ignore him so far, but that doesn't seem to be working."

"You've got to talk to him about it or it'll never get any better," Mercedes says "I had a student like that in my lab section last year, who always thought he knew more than I did and caused me a lot of trouble. I finally asked him what the problem was. After we talked for a while and I explained to him that I didn't appreciate his actions, things got a lot better. That's what you need to do."

"I suppose so. I hope it works."

"It will. Just use your natural brilliance and charm," says Maureen.

PROBLEM STUDENTS AND STUDENTS WITH PROBLEMS

The classroom and section meeting are the business end of education. Here students and staff deal together with the stuff of the intellect. Here also idiosyncrasies in both become apparent. Sometimes unusual behavior can be overlooked, but not if it disrupts the work of the group or upsets some of its members. Some problems you can handle yourself; more serious ones need to be referred to professionals competent in handling them. In some sense you are the "antennae of the system" and need to exert your influence in making it humane. Here are a few kinds of problem students you may encounter.

THE LOUD-MOUTH

There's a young man in the first row who talks too much: he blurts out answers before others have a chance, asks complicated questions off the subject being discussed, or holds forth at length on a pet topic. An occasional digression is fine, but if this behavior persists for several meetings you need to take action.

Start indirectly, trying to head off trouble by saying "Let's spread the answers around a bit," and obviously passing over the loud-mouth, or saying, "That's a fascinating topic; let's discuss it after class."

If this does not work, it is confrontation time. As class breaks up, ask him to stay for a minute. Then in the empty classroom, in an office with the door closed, or over coffee where you can talk privately, tell him you have a problem and ask for his help. (The problem is indeed yours; after all, talking too much is not causing any pain to him!) Tell him you value his participation and wish more students contributed. If his answers in class are generally good, say so. Do not criticize him but point out matter-of-factly the difficulty of involving everyone if someone dominates. If his knowledge of the subject is really advanced, should he be in another class?

When the point has been made and acknowledged, change the subject. At the end repeat your determination to involve everyone in the class.

THE POSSIBLE DATE

It's a situation that occurs in various sexual guises, but typically let's say you're a male recitation teacher of average libido, who can't help noticing that cute female with the turned-up nose who sits in the second row, asks good questions, and sometimes comes up after class with a comment. You find yourself drawn to her and wonder if you should ask her out for coffee, or dinner and a show. And see where it leads. Our advice is brief and it's official MIT policy: DON'T.

Heine, H., Richardson, P., Mattuck, A., Taylor, E., Brown, S., Olsen, A. and Russell, C. (1986). *The torch or the firehose? A guide to section teaching*. Massachusetts Institute of Technology.

You are not equals: this is a power relationship. This means that if you've misinterpreted things and she really doesn't want to go out with you, she may feel pressured and unhappy. If she does like you and you become involved with each other, the unequal relationship and possible sense of ulterior motives on either side can make for a lot of grief or trouble. Even if the two of you can manage it, others in the section will be suspicious and cynical, and your relationship with them will deteriorate.

So don't make a move until the semester is over and the grades come out. (If it's love at first sight and the two of you are desperate, she should at a minimum change sections.)

THE SILENT STUDENT

"You have the right to remain silent. Anything you say may be used against you." Students should have at least as much right to silence as those arrested for a crime. No one can or should force participation. Nevertheless, students who attend regularly but never speak up may be waiting for encouragement. Learn their names; when handing back assignments, compliment a particular solution if you can; ask them to come in during your office hour. After calling on three or four others in class, call on the silent one by name.

None of this may work. That is all right. Only gentleness is justified here.

THE DEPENDENT STUDENT

It may be flattering to have a student continually asking questions after class, filling your office hours, perhaps seeking extensive personal advice. It can also be a pain in the neck. If so, you have to decide where the problem is and act.

- If the student has too weak a background because of missing prerequisites, it's not your job to supply these by personal tutoring—recommend delaying the subject a semester, or a transfer to an easier version of the course if one is available.

- If the prerequisites are all there, but the student is just very weak in the subject, you do have some responsibility to help. However, it should be shared with the other tutoring services available (see the next sections). Set firm bounds on the amount of time you can spend and let the student know.

- Some students are "dependent types"—they like to be taken care of, or are used to leaning on some one. But this doesn't have to be you. Anyway, it's not good for them. Encourage them to stand on their own feet: "I could help you with this, but I think you'll learn more doing it by yourself."

- The student may be personally attracted to you—may want to be friends, or just enjoy spending time with you, possibly without realizing this explicitly. There's nothing wrong with this, but if you're unhappy about it, or cannot afford the time, there are many subtle ways to show that personal attention is unwelcome. Be businesslike, but tactful.

THE TROUBLED STUDENT

Students may come to you with personal or academic problems, because they like and trust you. Listen as you would listen to a friend who wanted to talk, and respond as you would to a friend, offering what advice you can.

If you feel more experienced guidance is called for—this will certainly be so if the problems are serious, with possibly deep-lying causes—then be wary of offering too much advice of your own. It's better to refer the student to one of the Institute's counseling resources, usually in the Office of the Dean for Student Affairs. Normally students are referred there by their advisors, and you should find out if the student has talked to his or her advisor, or would like to. You need to be tactful. In general, for serious cases, try to have the student make the appropriate appointment by phone while still in your office.

If it seems better initially not to involve the Dean's Office, in some cases the Campus Patrol can be the right resource—it enjoys excellent relations with students, the contact can be very informal, and it is helpful if the law may be involved.

A more formal resource is the Medical Department. Psychiatric referral is usually done through the Dean's Office, but you can call the Medical Department yourself if the case seems very serious or an emergency.

All of these resources are available to you for consultation. If you're not sure what the best thing to do is, call them up and ask their advice. They want you to, and you may be able to head off serious trouble.

If a life may be at stake, no matter how unlikely you think it is, act fast. One section leader noticed razor scratches on the wrists of a student who came to his office for help with a physics problem. He said nothing, but phoned the Dean's Office immediately afterwards. Within hours the student had called in, expressing appreciation that "someone would care".

ACADEMIC PROBLEMS

You should get in touch with students who do poorly on the first exam, or who miss a couple of homework assignments, to find out what the problem is. It is usually you who will have to do the seeking out, since students are embarrassed by poor grades or performance and thus feel awkward about seeing you. Many will try to pretend to themselves there is no problem, or optimistically hope that things will go better "when they get things together". Freshmen often behave this way, when after twelve years of success in school they find themselves for the first time in academic trouble and have to cope with the resulting internal and external pressures.

160

Your job is to confront these students gently with reality and get them to make sensible plans for their academic work. They may need suggestions on how to study and manage their time, as well as help with the course material. Encourage them to take advantage of the tutoring services available—those offered by the large freshman courses, the Black Students Union Tutoring Program, the dorm and fraternity tutors. Perhaps there is someone else in the section who lives nearby with whom they could study, or some upperclassman who can help.

If the problems seem serious, particularly if they extend to the other courses (be tactful about inquiring), you should contact the student's advisor. If the advisor doesn't seem like an appropriate first resource, it may be better to call the Undergraduate Academic Support Office (particularly for freshmen and undesignated sophomores), or where appropriate the Office of Minority Education. These offices do academic counseling and have programs designed to assist students with study skills and time management.

PROBLEMS WITH THE CLASS

In dealing with disagreement, confrontation, and inappropriate behavior, the new instructor should probably seek the advice or guidance of a more experienced person. Department heads and coordinators for teaching assistants have dealt with similar problems and can advise you on appropriate steps. New instructors are often afraid to share problems because they feel that these problems are their own fault or constitute a poor reflection on their teaching abilities. Similar problems arise continually, however, with new or experienced faculty, young or old, outstanding or less capable. In fact, students sometimes sense an inexperienced faculty member and believe they can "get away with" more because of the instructor's lack of experience. For these reasons, and for the reassurance it gives, it is usually best to discuss your interpersonal problems with someone who can help you.

DISAGREEMENT IN OR OUT OF THE CLASSROOM

Dealing with a student who disagrees politely, calmly, rationally is a pleasure. If you state your position openly, calmly, and rationally, the two of you are almost certain to reach a reasonable solution. It is with open hostility or conflict that most problems occur. Here are some suggestions for dealing with confrontation.

- If the confrontation occurs in a public setting, attempt to remove it to a private setting, e.g., an office. Often the confronter relies on the public nature of the attack and the encouragement of other students to press the argument.

- Listen carefully, openly, and professionally to the full criticism or grievance. Do not attempt to respond to allegations made during the narrative. Let the critic express all existing problems.

- Repeat the main points of the argument, as you understand them, to be sure both of you see the same issues.

- Accept any valid criticism and state your intended corrective action. Show a genuine willingness to compromise where you feel it is appropriate.

- Explain that you have different thoughts on the issue and would like an opportunity to express your point of view. State your opinions, and allow your critic to respond.

- If it appears that the issue cannot be resolved in a mutually satisfactory way, indicate regret that there remains a difference in view. Restate your position, making clear any action you intend to take. Indicate what recourse your critic has to other appeal channels.

Humphreys, L. and Wickersham, B. (1986). *A handbook of resources for new instructors at UTK.* Learning Research Center, University of Tennessee, Knoxville.

- Move in a polite and professional manner to close the conversation.

- If the critic becomes agitated, remain calm. Often your remaining calm will return the conversation to a more placid tone.

- It sometimes helps to ask a colleague to join in a confrontation, if the colleague can remain neutral and point out possible routes for solution of the problem. The student can also see the other person as a guarantee of fairness in the proceedings.

Summary

Some of the points contained in this section are:

- Head off persistent talkers with "Let's spread the answers out a bit" or with an invitation to further discuss a topic outside of class. (p. 158)

- Persistent talkers may need to be privately told that her/his participation is valued but that everyone in the class needs to participate. (p. 158)

- Do not date the students in your class. (p. 158)

- Do not force silent students to participate, but gentle encouragement is acceptable. (p. 159)

- Do not supply extensive personal tutoring to students who do not have the prerequisites for the course. (p. 159)

- Share tutoring with university tutoring services to students who are weak in the subject area. (p. 159)

- Encourage dependent students to stand on their own two feet. (p. 160)

- Be business-like and tactful to those clinging students who want to be friends. (p. 160)

- Listen to a student who comes to you with personal or academic problems and be prepared to make appropriate referrals to academic or other counseling centers. (p. 160)

- If there is even a remote possibility that a life is at stake, act at once. (p. 160)

- Gently confront those students with serious academic problems and offer them the phone numbers of offices where they can get tutoring or help, and give them "how to study" hints. (p. 161)

- Move openly hostile confrontations to a private setting. (p. 162)

- Deal with confrontations professionally; listen, accept valid criticism, be willing to compromise where appropriate, remain calm. (p. 162)

- A neutral colleague may be able to help during confrontations. (p. 163)

16
Professionalism

Steve comes bursting into Rosemary's Place, finds Maureen and Mercedes, and runs over, saying loudly, "I'm so disgusted!"

"Guess what!" he half-shouts.

"What?" they both reply.

"I just finished grading my students' midterms, and boy, are they awful. I can't believe anyone is this stupid."

"How do you mean?" asks Mercedes.

"Well, how about the guy who thought that the Articles of Confederation were a colonial marriage license?"

"Pretty bad, pretty bad, but you might want to keep it down. Some of your students might be here," says Maureen.

"So what?"

"Well, how would you like it if your stats professor came running in to a bar, screaming about how dumb you were? Nice, huh?"

"Hmmm. Hadn't thought about that. But, look, we're not faculty. We're only TAs. We don't get paid enough to worry about things like that."

"It's not a matter of payment, Steve," says Mercedes, "it's a matter of trust. The students in your class trust you to keep a professional attitude and to keep things like grades and records confidential. It's probably a law, too."

"It is a law," says Maureen, "but it's also a way of doing business. Sure, everybody exchanges stories about weird exam answers or funny sentences in papers, but you shouldn't make a big public deal about them. Just be cool."

"OK, OK, I hear you. Speaking of my stat professor, do either of you know anyone who tutors in stats? I need some real help."

"How much are you willing to pay?" asks Mercedes.

"It's not a matter of payment; it's a matter of desperation. How much do you want?"

PROFESSIONALISM

Graduate teaching assistants are academic anomalies, assuming the role of faculty when teaching and, then, reversing roles to become students when taking classes themselves. GTAs are neither fish nor fowl. They are frequently expected to put on and take off the roles of teacher and student, one hour being the instructor and the next the pupil.

Much of the relationship between teaching assistants and students is simply a matter of common sense. Undergraduates expect a GTA to conduct a class with the same professionalism as a faculty member. Behavior that is quite acceptable in a graduate seminar might be wholly inappropriate while teaching an undergraduate class. Discussing departmental faculty, other GTAs and their classes, assignments, grading, and course policies, as well as socializing with students outside of class, for example, are very much a part of the graduate student, but singularly unacceptable classroom conduct. Many other standards vary from department to department. While defining the teaching role is not usually difficult, it is, nonetheless, important.

Neither Fish nor Fowl

Humphreys, L. and Wickersham, B. (1986). *A handbook of resources for new instructors at UTK.* Learning Research Center, University of Tennessee, Knoxville.

PROFESSIONALISM AND CONFIDENTIALITY

Avoid discussing marks gained by students in public circles, especially with other students. Don't give out one student's marks to other students, in fact avoid giving out final marks at all. This function is carried out by the University, which officially notifies the students of their grades. The Department also posts unofficial final grades for each course on the bulletin board near the departmental offices on the first floor.

It is totally unprofessional to discuss publicly or gossip about the lecturers or your peers. TAs certainly get to know their lecturers well, but don't fall into the gossip trap.

Do not hustle the boys or girls in your class. Not nice! Infatuations do occur, and even true love, but an *obvious* affair will leave the class suspicious of your motives and your ability to treat everyone fairly, even if you are scrupulously honest about assigning marks. The possibility of legal action based on accusations of harassment should be borne in mind. Take care!

Humphreys, L. and Wickersham, B. (1986). *A handbook of resources for new instructors at UTK.* Learning Research Center, University of Tennessee, Knoxville.

ACADEMIC INTEGRITY

Scholarship is at home only in an atmosphere of honest practices by both students and faculty. All members of the academic community should conduct themselves in a straightforward and honorable manner. Study, instruction, evaluation, and research can flourish well only in such an environment.

Academic integrity is a joint endeavor. Faculty should make appropriate preparations for all student-teacher encounters, meet classes as scheduled, evaluate students' work fairly and impartially, and be prompt for prearranged conferences and regularly scheduled office hours. Inappropriate language in the classroom, off-color remarks or jokes in class as well as in personal conferences, and frequent deviations from the course topic have no proper place in the teaching academy. In turn, students should fulfill in a reasonable way the requirements and expectations of the course as stated by the instructor.

Within this shared enterprise, instructors have another, rather heavy, responsibility, that of making certain students can function in an atmosphere free of academic dishonesty. Students need to know that if they work honestly, they will not suffer because of those who do not. Challenging a student you think may have cheated or plagiarized is not pleasant. If you feel uncomfortable in this area of responsibility, a thoughtful discussion of the topic on pages 136-137 in McKeachie's (1978) *Teaching Tips*, as well as Chapter 13, "Situations," in Eble's (1976) *The Craft of Teaching*, may be helpful.

SEXUAL HARASSMENT

Reprinted below are two statements regarding sexual harassment. The first is from the Equal Employment Opportunity Commission of the U.S. Government, and is from their final set of guidelines making sexual harassment an act of discrimination under Title VII of the Civil Rights Act. The second is from a 1981 memorandum from Dr. Melvin A. Eggers, Chancellor of Syracuse University, to the University community, and is reprinted here with his permission.

Sexual harassment is defined by the EEOC as:

> "Unwelcome sexual advances, requests for sexual favors, and other verbal or physical conduct of a sexual nature . . . when (1) submission to such conduct is made either explicitly or implicitly a term or condition of an individual's employment, (2) submission to or rejection of such conduct by an individual is used as the basis for employment decisions affecting such individual, or (3) such conduct has the purpose or effect of unreasonably interfering with an individual's work performance or creating an intimidating, hostile, or offensive work environment."

Chancellor Eggers writes:

> "The academic community depends on the integrity of its members to maintain an environment in which all may function free of intimidation. Any faculty and staff members who would use the power and authority of their offices to achieve personal ends would corrupt the university. Sexual harassment is recognized as a means of limiting educational and professional opportunities, particularly of women."

Summary

Some of the points contained in this section are:

- Do not discuss departmental faculty, other teaching assistants and their classes, assignments, grading, or course policies. (p. 166)

- Do not socialize with students outside of class. (p. 166)

- Do not discuss student marks in public. (p. 167)

- Do not give out one student's marks to another student. (p. 167)

- Do not hustle the students in your class. (p. 167)

- Appropriately prepare for all student-teacher encounters. (p. 168)

- Meet classes as scheduled and keep scheduled office hours. (p. 168)

- Evaluate students' work fairly and impartially. (p. 168)

- Do not use inappropriate language or tell off-color jokes. (p. 168)

- Do not frequently deviate from the course topic. (p. 168)

- Be sure that students can function in an atmosphere free of academic dishonesty. (p. 168)

- The piece on sexual harassment should be read in its entirety. (p. 169)

17
Office Hours and Tutoring

Thursday afternoon. About 3:00. Maureen spies Steve on the Quad. She is puzzled.

"What are you doing here?"

"Oh, hi. Nothing much, just hanging out, enjoying the day, reading. Why?"

"Don't you have office hours now?"

"Yeah, but I blew them off. Nobody ever comes and it's too nice a day to be cooped up inside."

"Get up."

"What?"

"Get up. I'm taking you to your office."

"You're not my mother. What are you getting so excited about?"

"You have a responsibility to your students, and you're not living up to it. If they're not coming in, it just might be because they don't think you want them to. You've got to find a way to get them in. Invite one or two in just for a chat. See what happens. What if one of them is there now, and can't find you, and is desperate to ask you a burning question about the War of 1812?"

"Somehow I doubt it."

"I'll bet you someone's there."

"Oh, all right, but if no one's waiting for me, will you lay off?"

"Sure, and if there is, you'll never blow off office hours again. Deal?"

"Deal."

Steve marches confidently towards the history building, up the stairs, down the corridor towards his office, turns the corner . . . and sees Donna, a student in his intro American history class waiting outside.

"Oops. Hi, Donna. Just went out for a minute. Can I help you with something?"

"Um, yeah, if it's not too much trouble. I just have a couple of questions about the Battle of New Orleans. I can come back if you're busy," says Donna.

"No, no," chimes in Maureen, "he's not busy at all. I was just leaving. See you later, Steve."

"How did you know she was here?" asks Steve, frustrated.

"Call it a hunch. Besides, I'm a good friend of the writer. Bye!"

SMALL GROUPS:
TUTORIALS AND OFFICE HOURS

GROUP TUTORIALS

In some courses, in addition to having lectures and recitations, the students in a recitation section are further subdivided into several tutorial groups of 4-5 each, meeting once a week with a tutor who grades their problem sets and gives further assistance.

Conducting such a tutorial is an excellent way to start out with a course—you'll be close to the students and will perceive at first hand the sort of difficulties they have. It's a good way to start out in teaching, too—problems of getting acquainted and interaction are much less troublesome. But don't think that a small group makes them automatically disappear. Some tutors seem to end up lecturing to three students as if they were teaching 300.

RUNNING THE TUTORIAL

Assuming you've gone (as you should) to the lectures and recitations, you'll probably feel it your duty to clear up difficulties students had with poor explanations there. Do so, but don't spend all your time on this. Reinforce your explanations by working problems with them. There are different ways to do this.

One way is for everyone to contribute ideas, while you act as secretary at the board. This way they interact and get to know each other, and it's all the more social.

Or you can have students work individually, at their seats or the board, and you offer individual help. Maybe at the end one of them explains to the others. Working at their seats has the advantage that they have something to carry away with them; working at the board means they can see each other's work. Do both.

In general, try to keep the hour varied—some of this, some of that, but emphasizing whatever seems to work best with the particular group. Encourage them to keep track of difficulties during the week and bring them in. What bothers one student is likely to be a problem for others also.

Handling students of widely varying ability in a small tutorial is difficult. Your primary responsibility has to be to the ones having troubles. The others can help them, or work on more difficult things while you help them.

THE TUTOR AND THE RECITATION TEACHER

The divided responsibility causes problems. If you're running a small tutorial, you will probably feel closer to the students than to the lecturer or recitation teacher. Be tactful however about blaming the lecturer or recitation teacher for the students' troubles: "This point seemed to confuse some of you...", not "R _____ sure did a lousy job of explaining this..."

Heine, H., Richardson, P., Mattuck, A., Taylor, E., Brown, S., Olsen, A. and Russell, C. (1986). *The torch or the firehose? A guide to section teaching.* Massachusetts Institute of Technology.

The recitation teacher for a section which also has tutorials may feel somewhat distant from the students, since someone else is grading their problem sets and clearing up their confusions. Sometimes the tutor is felt to be sitting as a silent critic in the recitation. That's bad. Students should see recitation teacher and tutor working together in the classroom. The tutor should speak up in recitation if there's a suggestion to be made, and the recitation teacher should encourage this.

The teacher and tutor should meet regularly—weekly, or at least biweekly—to discuss what sort of errors students are making on the problem sets and what sort of troubles they are having with the course in general. Conveying the complaints of the students is an important responsibility, since the feedback provided can be a significant influence on the course.

INDIVIDUAL TUTORIALS AND OFFICE HOURS

Some of the above applies also to one-on-one tutorial sessions with students, either by appointment, at a clinic where you sit in a room and help whoever comes in, or as part of your regular office hours. For this one-on-one tutoring the main points are

- Knowing your stuff

- Being a good listener: try to find out what the difficulty is——ask, or have the student try to do the work in front of you and watch what he or she does, or look at graded quizzes and problem sets.

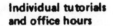

Individual tutorials and office hours

- Being flexible about trying one explanation after another, until you find one that works

- Having patience, patience, patience: no matter how frustrated you may get, try not to show it.

It is quite possible to handle several students at once in such individual sessions: one student can be thinking about what you've just said and working, while you are helping a second on a new problem. Always introduce them to each other. If you've just explained something to one student and another comes in with the same question, ask the first student to explain to the second, while you look on or help a third. It's good for everyone, and many students actually prefer to get help from other students rather than from the staff.

OFFICE HOURS

When and where your office hours will be held should be determined before your first class meeting and should be made perfectly clear to your students. Some departments require a specific number of office hours per week; in some courses, a larger amount of one-to-one interaction with students is desirable. If your department has no set requirements, it is reasonable to begin by establishing two to four hours a week for your office hours. Offer hours at different times during the week so that they will be convenient for students with varied schedules. For example, you should not have all of your hours on one day of the week, or even at the same hour on two different days. Obviously, it is difficult to set up office hours that will be convenient for all of your students. You should therefore also make yourself available to your students by special appointment. It is, of course, crucial that *you* show up for your office hours and appointments.

Students should also be told how to get in touch with you to make appointments or in emergency situations. This could be through your departmental mailbox or phone, or you could give your home phone number. Opinions on the advisability of giving out home telephone numbers vary. Do what feels comfortable to you.

What goes on during office hours depends on the subject matter of the course and on your attitudes towards the situation. If you have a receptive attitude toward your students, then getting to know them on a one-to-one basis during office hours creates a rapport which will carry over into the classroom. Some instructors find it helpful to require each student to make an initial office visit, perhaps after the first assignment has been handed in. This provides an opportunity to get to know the students better and also encourages them to avail themselves of your office hours. Another technique is to hold group office hours or review sections before exams or major assignments, but these should never take the place of a student's opportunity to see the instructor privately.

Wolke, Robert A. (Ed.) (1984). *A handbook for teaching assistants*. (2nd edition). Office of Faculty Development, University of Pittsburgh.

COUNSELING STUDENTS INDIVIDUALLY

A. OFFICE HOURS

Instructors at ODU are responsible for setting aside specific office hours so that other faculty members and students may confer with them. If the GTA has no office, he/she will need to schedule particular rooms for such activities. These hours should be posted on the instructor's office door and given to the department secretary. Listed below are some guidelines for office consultations.

1. Stop whatever you are doing and give the student your full attention. Help the student state the purpose of his/her visit by asking, "What can I do for you?" This avoids the possibility of engaging in guessing games, wasting time and addressing the incorrect issue.

2. Common problems arising in office counseling situations are students' concerns and complaints about grades, assignment deadlines or test dates. Be prepared for these types of requests by finding out the department's policies concerning assignments that are submitted late, exams that are missed, and grades that are challenged. It may be wise to briefly note these policies on the syllabus, for example, that "Unless a physician's note is provided, the grade for assignments turned in late will be lowered by one letter grade." It may be beneficial to discuss with experienced teachers how they respond to complaints and excuses from students, and how they gauge the seriousness of them.

3. One common student problem may be worded like this: "I study harder for this course than for all my other courses, but I just can't seem to pass the test." Encourage the student to examine the problem to determine where the breakdown is. Is the problem with attendance, notetaking, understanding of the material, doing reading assignments (before *and* after the lecture), study habits or time management? Sometimes, simple information on budgeting time or *study habits* can help (e.g. minimize distractions, peruse the whole chapter first then read in greater depth. Before closing the book, look back over the material that you just read and mentally summarize it. Jot down key points. Try to answer questions at the end of chapter. Note and look up unfamiliar words and maintain a vocabulary list.) Sometimes a simpler text from the library or professor can explain material in ways that can be a helpful backup to students having difficulty.

4. When students reveal or wish to discuss deeper psychological or emotional problems , it is probably desirable to advise them to get professional help, for example, to refer them to a counseling center. However, one should perhaps spend at least a few minutes listening to the problem rather than hastily dismissing the student by a referral. A sense of caring and concern should be conveyed, even if the problems and solutions lie outside one's area of professional training.

Jorgensen, S. (1987). *Instructional Resource Booklet for Graduate Teaching Assistants*. The Center for Instructional Services. Old Dominion University.

OFFICE HOURS

You should notify your students of your office hours, a minimum of two hours every week, at the first class. During office hours, you make yourself available to your students for individual help, and this has an obvious importance. A student will benefit more from detailed criticism of his own work on a one-to-one basis, than from a general discussion of writing problems in the classroom, and getting to know the students personally outside the context of the classroom is crucial not only for them, but also for you. The rapport you develop with the individual student in your office will carry over into the classroom, and the more relaxed each of them feels with you, the more relaxed and responsive will be the class as a whole.

Your students will appreciate any effort on your part to get to know them individually. Their teachers at high school would have known them at least by name. Suddenly they are away from home, at a large university, where they are often just a face in a lecture hall and an I.D. number. They rarely have the opportunity to get to know their professors; therefore you, as a TA in charge of a small class, are possibly their only close human contact with the academic powers-that-be. You are not only more accessible, but more approachable than a member of the faculty, and first year students who are experiencing university teething-troubles could start coming to you with personal and academic problems. You may find yourself having to deal with students who are bothered by anything from an unmanageable workload to chronic homesickness. By all means be sympathetic, but do not attempt to handle anything that is out of your depth. Few TAs are trained social workers, and you should refer students with serious problems to Counselling Services, where they will be put in touch with someone qualified to deal with a wide variety of personal difficulties.

Woodhead, J. (1979). *A manual for teaching assistants in the department of English.* Teaching Resource Office, University of Waterloo.

Summary

Some of the points contained in this section are:

- Keep the tutorial hour varied: mix group work with individual work. (p. 172)

- Be tactful about blaming the lecturer or recitation teacher for problems the students are having. (p. 172)

- Be flexible about trying different explanations. (p. 173)

- Be patient. (p. 173)

- Determine your office hours before the first class and make them known to your students. (pp. 174, 175, 176))

- Offer office hours at different times to accommodate varied student schedules. (p. 174)

- Be available by appointment to students who can't make it to your regular office hours. (pp. 174, 176)

- Show up for all office hours and appointments. (p. 174)

- Tell students how to get in touch with you. (p. 174)

- Require students to make an initial office visit. (p. 174)

- Hold group office hours. (p. 174)

- Hold at least two office hours a week, but check with your department on the number of hours required. (pp. 174, 176)

- Stop whatever you are doing and give the student your full attention. (p. 175)

- Be prepared for complaints about grades, assignment deadlines and test dates by finding out your department's policies beforehand. (p. 175)

- Students sometimes need information on time-budgeting and study habits. (p. 175)

- Convey a sense of caring and listen to a student's problems before advising them to get professional help. (p. 175)

- Get to know your students individually. (p. 176)

- Do not attempt to handle serious personal problems; refer them to the proper support unit or counseling center. (p. 176)

18
Syllabi

A little after midterms, Mercedes finds out she's been assigned a new class for the Spring semester, one she's never taught before. That evening, she discusses the class with Steve and Maureen.

"That's great!" says Maureen. "That means they like what you're doing and trust you with another class. I'm so happy for you!"

"Yeah, it's really great. What are you going to be teaching?" asks Steve.

"It's an intermediate course in programming. The only thing is, all the old syllabi are so *bad*. Most times, there hasn't been one, and the ones that have been written don't say anything useful about the class. I'll have to go through and design a new syllabus. What should I say?"

"Well," says Maureen, "really all you need to do is to say everything you would want to know if *you* were taking the class. What are the course requirements? What's the textbook? When's the final? What're your office hours? Also, be sure to include an outline of the classes and what you'll be covering. It doesn't have to be more than a page or so, and just common sense."

"There's nothing worse than a bad course syllabus," adds Steve. "I had a religion course when I was an undergraduate and the professor just sort of seemed to float from one class to another with no real plan as to what we'd be covering. We had a syllabus, but all it said was the name of the course, the professor's name, and the textbook, and some vague stuff about 'the study of religion.' That was one of the worst classes I ever had."

"Even worse than stats?" Maureen says, grinning.

Steve growls. "Thanks a lot for reminding me. I gotta go study. Bye."

PROFESSORS, STUDENTS, AND THE SYLLABUS

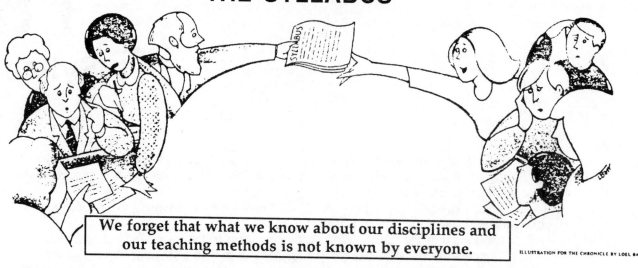

We forget that what we know about our disciplines and our teaching methods is not known by everyone.

ILLUSTRATION FOR THE CHRONICLE BY LOEL BARR

For the past two years I've been sitting in on the meetings of a committee charged with approving courses for the University of Maryland's general-education program. Very often the committee members leave those meetings mystified and exasperated. It's not that the courses proposed are inadequate; it's just that the syllabi submitted with the proposals are so often virtually impossible to decode.

I've listened while a faculty member from a related discipline has tried to guess what a syllabus might possibly mean. I've seen carefully worded letters from the dean requesting clarification—and then looked on as the committee has tried to relate a three-page response to the original syllabus. The committee has even developed a new cover sheet for all proposals, which requests detailed information about objectives and asks for samples of text questions and paper assignments. Yet sufficiently informative syllabi are still so rare that when one appears it elicits audible sighs of relief around the conference table.

The syllabi our committee gets are not much different from the ones I've picked up at conferences or seen attached to grant proposals. In other words, I don't believe the problem is local or idiosyncratic; rather, it seems to be basic to the teaching endeavor. We keep forgetting that what we know—about our disciplines, about our goals, about our teaching methods—is not known (or agreed upon) by everyone. We seem to assume that our colleagues and our students will intuitively be able to reconstruct the creature we see in our mind's eye from the few bones we give them in the syllabus.

The worst syllabi seem to fall into one of two categories.

The "listers" merely specify which books or chapters will be read during which weeks, without a hint about the principles behind the selection. The most puzzling of this type assign chapters in the textbooks in an order considerably different from the order intended by the authors. At best, such modification gives students the impression that the teacher is improving on the original organization for some as yet unrevealed purpose; at worst, it gives students the idea that one structure is no less logical or coherent than another, and that all parts are interchangeable and equally valid.

Rubin, S. (1985). Professors, Students and the Syllabus. *Chronicle of Higher Education*, August 7.

The "scolders" give brief descriptions of content and lengthy sets of instructions detailing what will happen if a student comes in late or leaves early, hands in a paper after the deadline, misses an exam, fails to follow the rules for margins and double-spacing, does not participate in class discussion. The scolders often sound more like lawyers than professors. Undoubtedly the syllabus as legal document has evolved because so often students demand that their teachers provide a set of rules, probably to give the students something concrete to cling to as they struggle with the content of the course. If even sophisticated scholars fall into the trap of equating quantitative data with significance, it's not surprising that students mistake the rules for the meaning.

Here are some questions our committee often finds unanswered even in wonderful syllabi for wonderful courses:

- Why should a student want to take this course? How does it make a difference as part of the discipline? How does it fit into the general-education program?

- What are the objectives of the course? Where does it lead, intellectually and practically? Students should be able to find out what they will know by the end of the course, and also what they will be able to do better afterward than before. Is the purpose of the course to increase their problem-solving abilities, improve their communication skills, sharpen their understanding of moral ambiguities, allow them to translate knowledge from one context to another? Why are the objectives important, and how will different parts of the course help students accomplish those objectives?

- What are the prerequisites? Students should be given some idea about what they should already know and what skills they should already have before taking the course, so they can realistically asses their readiness. Will they be expected to know how to compare and contrast, to analyze and synthesize, or will they be taught those skills during the course?

- Why do the parts of the course come in the order they do? Most syllabi note the order in which topics will be discussed, but make no attempt to explain the way the professor has chosen to organize the course. Sections of the syllabus are usually titled, but only infrequently are questions provided for students to help them put the reading assignments and homework into context.

- Will the course be primarily lectures, discussions, or group work? When a percentage of the grade is for "class participation," what does the professor expect from the students—regular attendance? questions? answers to questions? Will the students be given alternative ways to achieve success in the class, based on different learning styles?

- What is the purpose of the assignments? Students are frequently told how much an assignment will "count" and how many pages long it must be, but they are rarely given any idea about what it will demand of them or what the goal is. Will students be required to describe, discuss, analyze, provide evidence, criticize, defend, compare, apply? To what end? If students are expected to present a project before the class, are the criteria for an excellent presentation made clear?

- What will the tests test?—memory? understanding? ability to synthesize? To present evidence logically? To apply knowledge in a new context?

- Why have the books been chosen? What is their relative importance in the course and in the discipline? Is the emphasis in the course on primary or secondary materials and why?

"Well," you may say, "the syllabus isn't the course—everything will be made clear as the semester progresses." Or, "I can't ask my overworked secretary to type a 12-page syllabus." Or, "Students are interested only in the numbers—of books, of pages to read, of written assignments, of questions on the exam." Or, "A syllabus with all that information is too static—it doesn't allow me the flexibility to be creative on the spur of the moment." Maybe those are relevant objections—and maybe they are excuses for badly thought-out, hurriedly patched-together efforts. Whatever the rationale, I believe that the inadequate syllabus is a symptom of a larger problem—the lack of communication between teachers and students.

Most of the latest reports on undergraduate education have in common the criticism that faculty members and students no longer seem to be connecting. Our students do not seem to be involved in learning, they say. We seem to have lost the ability to create a shared community of values; we have substituted diversity for coherence and cannot find our way back to integrating principles. However, these reports all seem to ignore a very real wish among students and faculty members to find a place of meeting.

In 1982-83, Lee Knefelkamp of the University of Maryland asked 217 faculty members at eight colleges what they worried about most the first day of class. Their three most common concerns were, "Will the students get involved?" "Will they like me?" "Will the class work well as a class?"

When 157 students at those institutions responded to the same question, their three most common concerns were, "Will I be able to do the work?" "Will I like the professor?" "Will I get along with my classmates?"

The notion of relationship between teachers and students and material to be learned is clear in the answers from both groups. However, when the faculty members were asked what they thought students worried about the first day of class, they responded, "Will I get a good grade?" "Will the work be hard?" "Will the class be interesting?" When the students were asked what they thought teachers worried about, they generally couldn't answer the question at all.

The survey showed that there was a real desire on the part of both students and teachers for connectedness but neither group realized that the other shared that desire. If the participants on both sides don't understand how to develop their relationship, learning will be diminished.

The syllabus is a small place to start bringing students and faculty members back together, of course, and its improvement is not the revolutionary gesture that curriculum reform seems to be. But if students could be persuaded that we are really interested in their understanding the material we offer, that we support their efforts to master it, and that we take their intellectual struggles seriously, they might respond by becoming more involved in our courses, by trying to live up to our expectations, and by appreciating our concern.

Then the real work of learning can begin.

ISP 500 COMPUTER PROGRAMMING FOR INFORMATION SERVICES
Janes
Summer 1987

Syllabus

COURSE OBJECTIVES

Students will be introduced to computer programming through the use of Turbo Pascal, a very fast version of the Pascal language which we will be using on IBM PCs, but which is also available for Apple machines. Pascal is gaining wide acceptance as an educational language due to its intuitive nature and its modular structure. Pascal is a structured programming language and will be taught as such.

In addition, some background and history of computing will be given, with attention paid to computer jargon, elementary use of microcomputers, and other programming languages.

No prior programming experience is expected or required.

OUTLINE OF CLASSES

Jun 30	T	Introduction, DOS	1, Apx 6,7
Jul 1	W	The Turbo System	Apx 8,9,10
2	R	Pascal Begins: Variables, Types, Identifiers	2
6	M	Algorithms	
7	T	More Pascal: CONST, Types Again, Standard Functions, Arithmetic	3
8	W	PROCEDURE	4
9	R	**Lab**	
13	M	PROCEDURE 11: The Adventure Continues	5
14	T	Decisions	6
15	W	Boolean Uses	7
16	R	**Lab**	
20	M	Loops	8
21	T	FUNCTION	9
22	W	Yet More Data Types: Ordinal, Enumerated, Subrange, Structured	10
23	R	**Lab**	
27	M	Methodology	11
28	T	Records	14
29	W	Files	13
30	R	**Lab**	
Aug 3	M	History of Computing	
4	T	Other Programming Languages	
5	W	Text Processing Applications	
6	R	Advanced Topics	

Lab sessions will be held each of 4 Thursdays to work through problems, answer questions and explore applications of material covered previously.

TEXT

Savitch, Walter J., *An Introduction to the Art & Science of Programming: Turbo Pascal Edition*, Benjamin/Cummings Pub Co 1986 (pb)

COURSE REQUIREMENTS AND GRADING

Small assignments	10
Algorithm Design Assignments	20
Project	70

One or two small assignments will be given early in the course. The bulk of the grade will be based on the project, which will be completed in pieces throughout the summer. Each piece will be graded individually on the basis of *that piece* alone, then a final grade will be assigned to the large program as a whole. That final grade will be 20 of the 70 points allotted. Algorithm Design Assignments will be given throughout the summer.

Programs will be graded according to these criteria:

Logic/Operation	40
Documentation	20
Output Format	10
Error Control	10
User Concerns	10
Elegance/Misc	10
Total	100

COURSE AND GRADING PHILOSOPHY

A final grade of B will be given for satisfactory graduate-level work in this course. All other grades will be in relation to this standard.

All work submitted is assumed to be the expression of original ideas of the individual. Use of a programming language can, at times, seriously constrict the range of possible expressions. It is therefore very important that students take meticulous care in ensuring that assignments which have been discussed with others do not wind up looking exactly the same when submitted.

WHAT DID YOU PUT IN YOUR SYLLABUS?

One way to reach students early is to put in writing and then discuss the course policies, requirements, tests, and assignments. Since your syllabus is already written, use this checklist to test its adequacy. Give yourself *one point* for each element you have included.

_____	1.	Your name, title, office number, office telephone, office hours, and where to leave messages.
_____	2.	Course by number, section, title, meeting days and times, room and building.
_____	3.	Pre-requisite(s) for the course.
_____	4.	Description of the course.
_____	5.	✓Course goals or objectives.
_____	6.	Required purchases: texts and supplies.
_____	7.	Space for names and telephone numbers of at least two classmates.
_____	8.	Due dates for major assignments; place, date, time of final exam.
_____	9.	✓Grading standards and criteria.
_____	10.	✓Policy regarding P/NP, I, W marks.
_____	11.	✓Policy regarding academic dishonesty.
_____	12.	✓Policy regarding attendance.
_____	13.	✓Policy regarding late assignments.
_____	14.	Topics to be covered in sequence with dates.
_____	15.	Reading assignments and dates due.

Not all elements listed here will be found in every syllabus. A syllabus can be much more than a list; it can introduce the course to the students in a number of creative ways. (See the article, "Professors, Students and the Syllabus" in the August 7, 1985 *Chronicle of Higher Education*) The University, however, does require that "students . . . be informed of the requirements, standards, objectives, and evaluation procedures at the beginning of each individual course." The Faculty Senate recommends that course policies (including those marked with an ✓ above) should be in written form.

Scoring: 15-14: Great! Send us a copy
          13-12: Good job
          11-10: What did you leave out?
       9 or lower: Do you want a major overhaul?

What did you put in your syllabus? (1985). *Teaching at UNL*, 7 (1). University of Nebraska-Lincoln.

19
Humor in the Classroom

"I don't get it," complained Maureen one night towards the end of the semester. "I spend lots of time preparing my classes, working on the assignments, grading papers, and still this class just sits there. We do get into some good discussion, but there's something missing. I've never had this problem before."

"Try spicing it up with some jokes and stuff," offers Steve.

"Jokes? That's really not my style. Do you think it will work?"

"Well, I've had a couple of professors who used humor quite effectively. It keeps people interested, perks them up a bit and makes the time go faster. On the other hand, it can also be a disaster."

"That's what I'm worried about. Like what?"

"Well, have you ever been in a class where the professor tried to tell a joke or a funny story or make a humorous aside, and everybody *knew* he was trying to be funny, and wasn't, and everybody just got sort of embarrassed?"

"Yeah. You see, that's what I mean. I don't think I can be funny in front of my class. I try to project a pretty formal image when I'm teaching and if I start doing stand-up routines, it would really clash."

"Well, by all means don't try it unless you feel comfortable with it. I've got to give my lecture in a couple of weeks, and I'm not trying to make it a comedy routine, but I'd like to have them enjoy it as well as make them think about the material and remember it."

"Good luck. If you can do that, you're better off than a lot of faculty around here."

"I know. Maybe they'll hire me full-time next year. I could be a star faculty member."

"You have to pass stats first. How's that coming?"

"Be quiet and pass the popcorn."

187

HUMOR IN THE CLASSROOM?
YOU GOTTA BE KIDDING!

Is there a place for humor in the classroom? Of course there is. There is a place for humor in almost all human experiences. Two exceptions are funerals and the preparation of income tax forms. Those tend to get real sticky. But humor, being a very important part of life, does have a place in the teaching-learning experience.

Let me tell you a story about a psychologist who does a crazy thing in one of his courses. (I'm told that you don't have to be crazy to be a psychologist, but it helps.) When he gets to the topic of *conditioning* he comes to class dressed like a turkey: a mask on his face, a droopy red beret on his head, feathers attached to a robe that has TURKEY written in large letters across the back. The students are startled and then they crack up. When he asks them to condition his behavior in some way, they jump to it eagerly. Then, when they are unable to succeed, he makes a number of educational points about conditioning, and they remember. It's a hilarious situation and the students learn a lot—through humor.

I'm not saying that the classroom should be a showcase for new comedy acts or that humor is appropriate for every situation. Humor is a tool to be used when it is needed to achieve specific purposes. There are several important considerations to keep in mind when using it. I'll get to those in a moment. But first let me tell you that there may be some good reasons why a teacher might *not* want to use humor at all.

In some instances, course objectives and the nature of the subject matter may not lend themselves to a humorous approach. It is difficult, for example, to find something funny to say about the Crusades or the Spanish Inquisition. If you are basically a light-hearted person, you may want to take pains to play such topics straight.

Hurley, C. (1985). Humor in the classroom? You gotta be kidding! *EKU-Teaching,* 2 (1). Eastern Kentucky University.

An individual's personality and teaching style may not be consistent with the use of humor. I have known some teachers who seemed to believe that smiling indicated a weakness in character. They were good teachers in spite of that. They were well-prepared, they were professional in their approach, but for the life of me, I believe they must have been weaned on pickle juice. Also, there are thousands of teachers across this land with great personalities and a keen sense of humor who go about the business of changing lives and seldom use humor as a teaching tool. Humor is not a necessity.

Some students may misunderstand the use of humor. They may get the idea that because the teacher is not interested in inflicting pain on the student that she or he is not totally serious about the course. This misconception can usually be cleared up early in the course with a couple of quizzes or assignments that allow a teacher to demonstrate the ability and desire to evaluate student progress fairly and accurately.

A student fighting for dear life to hold onto a D in a course might resent the use of humor. Furthermore, a few students like that may just be looking for a place to lay blame: everyone *knows* that a teacher who jokes or cuts up with students can't be serious about teaching. This erroneous belief can be dispelled by making sure that course objectives are communicated clearly and that students know what is expected of them and how they are going to be evaluated. This is what good teachers do anyway, of course; it's nothing special that you have to do to support humor.

Now, if you think that humor *does* have a place in your classroom, consider some of the good uses to which it can be put.

Humor can help relieve tension on the part of the student. Of course, some tension can be useful; it keeps a person alert and helps bring out the best performance. However, too much tension can get in the way of learning. We've all known students who have performed poorly even though they knew the material and could work the problems.

Humor can help students remember. It provides a hook on which to hang important facts and concepts. Several years ago I did some informal classroom research which supported this idea. I purposely related humor to several of the major points in the subject matter, but not to others. I was amazed to see on the subsequent test the high percentage of correct answers by students on those questions covering the points on which humor had been used.

Humor can make an otherwise relatively uninteresting class more enjoyable. It is human nature to be attracted to those things we enjoy and to develop avoidance tendencies regarding those things that make us uncomfortable. Humor does not replace good teaching; it should be used to enhance the subject matter as herbs and spices are used to make the flavor of food more interesting.

Please don't misunderstand me. You are not employed to be an entertainer, even though some students seem to expect this and rate you low if you don't do a dog-and-pony show. Students need to know that learning is not always totally enjoyable. Sometimes there is no way to avoid hard work. (Lord knows, I've tried, and earning a living by trying to be funny isn't any easier than teaching.) If a university is doing what it is supposed to be doing, a student must expect to put in many hours in laboratories and libraries and to engage in just plain, hard studying. This revelation came to me in a vision when I was finishing my third year as a freshman.

Even though humor can be put to very good use, considerable care must be exercised in applying it in class.

Humor should not be forced. It should be used only by teachers who are comfortable with it. If it is not a natural thing for you to do, forget it; you certainly don't have to use it to be a good teacher. Go about planning without regard to humor; after your objectives are established and your lectures and student activities are designed, then consider humor. If a lot of planning is required to work it in, you may be trying too hard and the results may not seem spontaneous and natural. It is important for students to see you as a person who is genuinely funny at times, not as a person straining to be funny.

I remember one class when I used humor without planning to. We were discussing the stages in psychomotor skill development, how it progresses from imitation to naturalization, when the skill might be performed regularly without even thinking about it. (This can be dangerous when operating certain kinds of machinery. My wife has driving so naturalized that she can make out a grocery list and change her shoes while driving 55 m.p.h.) I was using walking as an example, explaining how babies look around, notice other people walking on their hind legs, and start to imitate—first holding onto something and then soloing. Since their muscles are not accustomed to this and their center of gravity is high, their movement is tottering at first. I became aware that the class was cracking up before I realized that I had been waddling across the room with my arms up for balance and my head doddling, picking up my feet and placing them down in almost the same position in a flat-footed manner. I must have looked like a cross between a wounded hippo and a duck with a back problem. Well, I can tell you it was worth it––the students did remember the stages in psychomotor development.

Sometimes even good applications of humor will not be received well by every last student, no matter how careful you are. Remember the psychologist I mentioned earlier? At the end of one of his courses, a student wrote on the evaluation form: "The turkey bit you did was ridiculous. Why did you bother to dress up in that outfit? You didn't look or act any different than usual." Alas, there's one in almost any crowd, but don't let that stop you from trying humor.

Timing is very important for humorous effects. The arrangement of critical points of a story and the effective use of pauses are the most important aspects in the delivery of material, the things that make the difference in whether it is funny or not. You've heard people say, "It's the way he tells it that makes it funny" or "Some people can tell a story, some can't." They're talking about timing more than anything else.

The story's placement in the class period should be considered carefully. It's like playing the cymbals in a band: how you play them is important, but *when* you play them is critical. Humor sets a certain tone and changes the mood of a group. If you don't want the mood changed, don't use humor. A story at the right time can enhance your teaching, but the same story at the wrong time can detract from your purpose. Considering *why* you are using a humorous spot will help with its placement.

That reminds me of something that happened down home. The sheriff was after an old boy for bootlegging, and they were engaged in a high-speed automobile chase. All of a sudden, when he just about had the boy caught, the sheriff's new car came due for its 5,000 mile check-up and, aw shucks, he had to stop and get the oil changed. Poor timing caused him to lose the criminal.

Humor is a complex phenomenon. Its use often requires the receiver to see people and things in unfamiliar patterns. That's one reason why something might be funny. Providing a sudden twist in the use of facts and ideas is another. That's how many comedians make their living. However, this same behavior in teachers may cause some students to see the teacher as unpredictable. This is OK as long as it doesn't generate anxiety or confuse a student to the point where it interferes with learning. Always keep an eye on your audience and be aware of how your behavior is affecting the behavior of those you are teaching. The teacher's behavior is the most important and most adjustable element in the teaching-learning transaction.

And please be careful to not poke fun at another person. Students don't deserve that. If someone must be the brunt of humor, use yourself. But don't do that to the point where you are putting yourself down; you don't deserve that, either.

As you plan for the use of humor, remember that it is difficult to justify a large amount of class time for jokes and stories. If a humorous item doesn't relate to the subject matter, you probably shouldn't use it. An exception might be something short right at the beginning of class to release tension and to gain students' attention. The humor you use should be spontaneous for the most part, not very time-consuming, and related to the subject in order to make a point.

One of the best professors I ever had was a master of this. He was a professor of the Old School. He commanded respect, he *looked* like a professor; even freshmen who didn't know the library from the bookstore could tell he was a professor. He considered learning to be something noble and the classroom to be a hallowed place. He had a profound command of his subject and his delivery held students on the edge of their seats. Humor?—He used it sparingly but effectively. After he introduced important facts and concepts, he might give a short anecdote to drive home a point or help relate the materials to the students' frame of reference. Often his humor was merely a matter of a well-turned phrase. I can still remember his saying, "Without a philosophy a person is lost—like someone who finds a rope and doesn't know whether he has found just a rope or has lost a horse," and "Write your sentences so tightly that when you pluck them they ring like a banjo." Once after a seminar he said, "We kicked up some rabbits here tonight and we've chased several of them, but I'm not sure we've caught any yet."

That's what I mean about humor as flavoring in teaching. It doesn't have to be a hilarious episode; it may only be a matter of a couple of words or a shift in gesture. This professor made me proud that I was going into teaching and he taught me many valuable things. More than anyone else, he taught me that a teacher can be well-prepared and serious about the subject, that high performance can be demanded of students, yet humor can be used effectively in helping students grow and develop in positive ways.

Carl Hurley describes himself as "a professional speaker/humorist—I never know which until I'm finished." He was Professor of Industrial Education in EKU's Department of Curriculum and Instruction for eight years before leaving to devote full-time to speaking engagements and management seminars throughout the U.S. and Canada. His first comedy album, "Makin' Change," has just been released and is available in the EKU Bookstore.

Summary

Some of the points contained in this section are:

- Use humor when it is needed to achieve specific purposes. (p. 188)

- Don't use humor with topics that do not lend themselves to humor. (p. 188)

- Don't use humor if your personality and teaching style are not consistent with its use. (p. 189)

- Don't use humor when students could misunderstand its use. (p. 189)

- Use humor to relieve student tension. (p. 189)

- Use humor to make a relatively uninteresting class more enjoyable. (p. 189)

- Don't consider humor as a replacement for good teaching (p. 189)

- Don't force humor. (p. 190)

- Always watch your audience and note how your behavior is affecting them. (p. 190)

- Don't poke fun at another student. (p. 191)

Conclusion

Steve, Mercedes, and Maureen gather for one last time before Christmas at Maureen's apartment. They exchange presents, drink a little eggnog, and talk.

"Well, we made it," says Maureen. "Here's to the end of the semester and the beginning of break!" They toast.

"It's been kind of tough at times," says Mercedes, "but I've really enjoyed myself this year. I'm looking forward to next semester, too. That's going to be an exciting course."

"Yeah, I've had a good time, too," says Steve. "I wasn't sure how I was going to feel about teaching, but after I got over the initial nerves, it was fine."

"Nerves? *Nerves*?! I thought you were just breezing your way through," says Maureen.

"Oh, uh, well, I *was* nervous; I just didn't want to show it," Steve stammers. "Pretty dumb, huh?"

"Not at all. The only thing that matters is that you learned something in the process."

They then turn and address you, the reader.

"We hope we've helped you, too. We know what it feels like to contemplate that first day in front of a class," says Maureen. "Just be yourself. You're going to be fine. No one's ever died from first-day jitters. Actually, the fact that you're nervous is a good sign. It shows you're concerned and want to do a good job. That's a good start. Look, if Steve can do it, anyone can."

"Hey!"

"Quiet. It's Mercedes' turn."

"Thanks, Maureen. The best advice I can give you after finishing my first class is just to do it. You can read every book ever written on teaching, go to seminars, be videotaped, and do all that other stuff, and that will certainly help, but the only way to be a good teacher is to be a teacher. If your first class is a disaster, and it might be, just go back the second day and try again. You'll get better. And don't be afraid to ask for help. It's not an admission of weakness, it's just a desire to improve. You will."

"Can I talk now?" asks Steve.

"I suppose so."

"Gee, thanks. I guess I agree with these guys, which is kind of scary. All I want to say is that other teachers are there, too, and you should seek them out if you have problems or questions. The three of us have helped each other a lot this year, and you should talk to other people, too."

"That's sweet," says Mercedes.

"It was," says Maureen. "How surprising. You're human, after all."

"I kept telling you so. Oh, by the way, I'm sure you're all dying to know how I did on my stat final, right?"

"I haven't been able to sleep all week thinking about it," says Maureen.

"*You* stay out of this. Well, you'll all be happy to know that I passed with flying colors, and I won't have to take any more statistics. Ever. I'm free!"

Mercedes asks gently, "Don't you have language requirements in your program?"

"Thanks for reminding me. Something else to panic about for four months."

"We all wish you the very best as you start teaching," says Maureen. "Teaching can be a tremendously rewarding experience, but like anything else, it takes practice to have the self-confidence to be good at it. As they say, the journey of a thousand miles begins with a single step. We hope your journey is a smooth one."

List of Sources

Cohn, C. and Buckley, J. (1977). *A TA's guide to Syracuse University.* Syracuse University.

Cotton, A. (1979). *Guidelines for teaching assistants in Geography.* Geography Department, Teaching Resource Office, University of Waterloo.

Crews, F. (1984). *The Random House handbook.* NY: Random House, Inc.

Davis, B.Gross (1987). *Preventing student academic dishonesty.* Office of Educational Development, University of California, Berkeley.

Diamond, N., Sharp, G. & Ory, J. *Improving your lecturing.* Office of Instructional Resources, University of Illinois at Urbana Champaign.

Ely, D. (1987, February). *Effective teaching techniques: lecturing.* Presentation at the Seminar on Teaching, Syracuse University

Funk, F. (1987, February). *Using class discussion as a teaching tool.* Presentation at the Seminar on Teaching, Syracuse University.

Gerlach, V. & Ely, D. (1980). *Teaching and media: A systematic approach.* (2nd ed.). NJ: Prentice-Hall.

Handbook for graduate teaching assistants. (1987). Office of Instructional Development, The Graduate School, University of Georgia.

Heine, H., Richardson, P., Mattuck, A., Taylor, E., Brown, S., Olsen, A. and Russell, C. (1986). *The torch or the firehose? A guide to section teaching.* Massachusetts Institute of Technology.

Humphreys, L. & Wickersham, B. (1986). *A handbook of resources for new instructors at UTK.* Learning Research Center, University of Tennessee, Knoxville.

Hurley, C. (1985). Humor in the classroom? You gotta be kidding! *EKU-Teaching,* 2 (1). Eastern Kentucky University.

Jorgensen, S. (1987). *Instructional resource booklet for graduate teaching assistants.* The Center for Instructional Services, Old Dominion University.

Loheyde, K. (1978). *TA-ing at Cornell: A handbook for teaching assistants.* Office of Learning and Teaching Services, Cornell University.

Morrow, R. (1976). What every TA should know. In *The TA at UCLA: A handbook for teaching assistants.* (1977-78). The Regents of the University of California.

Napell, S. (1978). Using questions to enhance classroom learning. *Education,* 99 (2).

Ory, J. (1987). Testing the test. *The teaching professor,* 1 (9), Madison, WI.: Magna Publications, Inc.

Palmer, S. (1983). The art of lecturing: A few simple ideas can help teachers improve their skills. *Chronicle of Higher Education*, April 13, p. 19.

Povlacs, J. (1986). 101 things you can do the first three weeks of class. *Teaching at UNL*, 8 (1). University of Nebraska-Lincoln.

Rollins, S. (1987). *Tips on teaching.* Instructional Development Center, Bryant College.

Rubin, S. (1985). Professors, Students, and the Syllabus. *Chronicle of Higher Education*, August 7.

What did you put in your syllabus? (1985). *Teaching at UNL*, 7 (1). University of Nebraska-Lincoln.

Wolke, Robert A. (Ed.) (1984). *A handbook for teaching assistants.* (2nd ed.). Office of Faculty Development, University of Pittsburgh.

Woodhead, J. (1979). *A manual for teaching assistants in the department of English.* Teaching Resource Office, University of Waterloo.

Index

Note: Indexed here are the readings themselves, not the dialogues or summaries, with one exception: the statement on plagiarism from the University of Tennessee at Knoxville reprinted in the summary of Chapter 12 (p. 144).

Figures in plain type are page numbers, in **bold italics** are entire chapters referring to the topic.

197

About the Editors

Joseph Janes, a native of Oneida Castle, New York, is a doctoral candidate in Information Transfer in the School of Information Studies at Syracuse University. He has taught at Syracuse University, at the State University of New York at Albany, and the University of North Carolina at Chapel Hill. Currently, he is serving as Research Assistant to the Vice President for Research and Graduate Studies at SU. Joe enjoys reading, food, SU basketball games, music, and bad 1950's Universal Studio's science-fiction films.

Diane Hauer, a native of Rochester, New York, is a doctoral candidate in Instructional Design, Development and Evaluation in the School of Education at Syracuse University. She spent two years teaching emotionally disturbed adolescents, was a teaching assistant at Boston University, and is currently on the staff of the Center for Instructional Development at Syracuse University. Diane is an ardent Boston Red Sox fan, enjoys reading, entertaining friends, attending hockey games, and would like to list more interests, but would have no free time in which to pursue them anyway.